Algebra Su[rvival]
Workbook
SECOND EDITION

by Josh Rappaport
author of the
Algebra Survival Guide

Algebra Survival Workbook
Second Edition

**Thousands of Problems to Sharpen Skills
and Enhance Understanding**

Published by:
Singing Turtle Press
942 Vuelta del Sur
Santa Fe, NM 87507

Tel: 1/505-690-2351
Fax: 1/512-682-0500
www.SingingTurtle.com
E-mail: info@SingingTurtle.com

SINGING
TURTLE
P R E S S

The publisher expresses heartfelt appreciation to Paul Obrecht for his superb technical consulting and mathematical typesetting services.
A big thanks, too, to David Cox for his digital background photos, all shot in Santa Fe, New Mexico.
Thanks — as always — to Sally Blakemore, for her inspired artwork, ongoing support, and joyful marimba music.
Last but not least, thanks to the author's family, for inspiration.

— Attention Teachers / Administrators —
For information on volume discounts to schools, visit us at: SingingTurtle.com
Or call us at the phone number above.

Contents

Welcome to the Workbook!

Flipping through this Workbook, you can see it's packed with thousands of practice problems ... and answers to every single one of them (not just to the odds!). But for whom is this Workbook intended, and how does one make optimal use of it?

This book is for EVERYONE who wants help LEARNING or TEACHING PRE-ALGEBRA and ALGEBRA 1. That means it's for TEACHERS, TUTORS, PARENTS, STUDENTS, HOMESCHOOLERS, precocious young MATH WHIZZES, ADULTS returning to school ... leaving anyone out? Let me know.

How does one use the Workbook? It's best used along with my *Algebra Survival Guide* (ASG), also published by Singing Turtle Press. That's because the Workbook's problem sets are keyed to the pages of the *Algebra Survival Guide*. If you have the Guide, you know that it provides clear instructions on how to do every problem set in this Workbook, along with conversational explanations of the concepts. If you don't have the Guide, get a copy now to reap the greatest benefit from this Workbook.

Here are some special ways the Workbook can help you!

➤ Each problem set focuses on just ONE SPECIFIC SKILL. I've found that children are most likely to succeed at algebra if they first learn a skill, then master it through PLENTY OF PRACTICE. This Workbook gives them that chance to understand and excel.

➤ Many problem sets use not only numbers and variables, but also SYMBOLS and FUNNY WORDS. The symbols and funny words are not just for entertainment. When children see symbols and words in algebraic rules and formulas, it gives them a way to GRASP THE FORMULA IN ITS MOST GENERAL SENSE. This helps them retain the concepts, for they understand them more deeply.

➤ Like the Guide, the Workbook teaches children not only WHAT TO DO, but also WHAT NOT TO DO. Learning the PITFALLS TO AVOID is as important as learning the correct algebraic procedures.

➤ The Workbook serves as a springboard for FUN AND CREATIVE PROJECTS. Example: Once children master a problem set, encourage them to make up a set of problems just like the ones they now understand. Then have them exchange problems with other children, or with their parents. Come up with your own extensions.

I'm confident that this Workbook will enhance your ability to teach or learn algebra. Best of luck on your ongoing trek through the *Algebra Wilderness!*

— Josh Rappaport

Which properties, if any, are shown by these statements — reflexive, symmetric, or transitive?

See ASG, pp. 9–11

1) $ab = ab$ _____
2) If $6x = 12$, then $x = 2$ _____
3) If $6x = 12$, then $12 = 6x$ _____
4) If $a = r$, and $r = q$, then $a = q$ _____
5) If $a = b$, and $g = h$, then $a = h$ _____
6) If $5b = a$, then $a = 5b$ _____
7) If $2x = y$, and $y = 4z$, then $2x = 4z$ _____
8) $m = n = p$ _____
9) If $m = m$, and $n = n$, then $m = n$ _____
10) If $5 \cdot 2 = 10$, then $10 = 5 \cdot 2$ _____

_____ %

Which properties, if any, are shown by these statements — associative, commutative, or distributive?

See ASG, pp. 12–15

1) $4(3 + 2) - 4 \cdot 3 + 4 \cdot 2$ _____
2) $4 \cdot (3 \cdot 2) = (4 \cdot 3) \cdot 2$ _____
3) $6 + 2 = 2 + 6$ _____
4) $7(x + y) = 7x + 7y$ _____
5) $m \cdot n = n \cdot m$ _____
6) $16 \div 2 = 2 \div 16$ _____
7) $x(y + z) = xy + xz$ _____
8) $x(y + z) = (x \cdot y) + z$ _____
9) $x \cdot (y \cdot z) = (x \cdot y) \cdot z$ _____
10) $12 + (a + b) = (12 + a) + b$ _____

_____ %

Which properties, if any, are shown by these statements — additive identity or multiplicative identity?

See ASG, pp. 17–18

1) $5 \cdot 1 = 5$ _____
2) $m + 0 = m$ _____
3) $7x \cdot 1 = 7x$ _____
4) $r \cdot 0 = r$ _____
5) $42c + 0 = 42c$ _____
6) $(a \cdot b) \cdot 0 = (a \cdot b)$ _____
7) $a + 1 = a$ _____
8) $a \cdot 1 = 1$ _____
9) $(4a + 3b) \cdot 1 = 4a + 3b$ _____
10) $(3m + 5n) + 0 = 3m + 5n$ _____

_____ %

To which sets of numbers, if any, do the following belong — natural (N), whole (W), or integer (I)?

See ASG, pp. 23–25

1) 4 _____
2) – 1 _____
3) 7 _____
4) 0 _____
5) – 12 _____
6) 14/3 _____
7) – 123 _____
8) 147 _____
9) 3.2 _____
10) 6/11 _____

11) 18,482 _____
12) 1 _____
13) – 8.5 _____
14) – 87 _____
15) 63.7 _____
16) 81 _____
17) – 81 _____
18) 6,351 _____
19) – 785 _____
20) – 10/3 _____

_____ %

To which sets of numbers, if any, do the following belong — rational (R) or irrational (I)?

See ASG, pp. 26–28

1) 82 _____
2) $\sqrt{5}$ _____
3) 7.63582196… _____
4) 1.125 _____
5) $\sqrt{13}$ _____
6) 4.12701270… _____
7) 2/9 _____
8) $\sqrt{2}$ _____
9) 61 _____
10) 4.444… _____
11) 43.121212… _____
12) 1.1024697… _____
13) 480/713 _____
14) 1/4 _____
15) π _____
16) 8.063258196… _____
17) 8.06325 _____
18) 14.0691436… _____
19) 1.111… _____
20) $\sqrt{24}$ _____

_____ %

Simplify using the same-sign rule.   See ASG, pp. 36–38

1)   + 2 + 1   _____   16)   – 16 – 9   _____
2)   + 4 + 3   _____   17)   + 21 + 21   _____
3)   – 6 – 4   _____   18)   – 21 – 18   _____
4)   + 1 + 7   _____   19)   – 15 – 15   _____
5)   – 8 – 4   _____   20)   + 17 + 17   _____
6)   – 1 – 2   _____   21)   + 6 + 3 + 5   _____
7)   + 7 + 6   _____   22)   + 8 + 4 + 2   _____
8)   + 6 + 9   _____   23)   – 6 – 3 – 7   _____
9)   – 7 – 3   _____   24)   + 10 + 8 + 6   _____
10) – 6 – 5   _____   25)   – 11 – 7 – 8   _____
11) + 11 + 8   _____   26)   – 14 – 1 – 5   _____
12) – 14 – 7   _____   27)   + 1 + 4 + 13   _____
13) – 9 – 12   _____   28)   + 3 + 16 + 8   _____
14) + 7 + 18   _____   29)   + 15 + 15 + 15   _____
15) + 15 + 2   _____   30)   – 8 – 16 – 32   _____

31) + 1 + 2 + 3 + 4   _____
32) – 2 – 4 – 6 – 8   _____
33) – 3 – 6 – 9 – 12   _____
34) + 4 + 8 + 12 + 16   _____
35) + 2 + 10 + 4 + 12   _____
36) – 6 – 7 – 8 – 9   _____
37) – 4 – 12 – 1 – 6   _____
38) + 13 + 8 + 4 + 1   _____
39) + 18 + 21 + 6 + 13   _____
40) – 8 – 7 – 1 – 17   _____
41) + 1 + 3 + 5 + 7 + 9   _____
42) + 2 + 6 + 5 + 1 + 4   _____
43) + 2 + 2 + 2 + 2 + 2   _____
44) – 8 – 3 – 1 – 4 – 9   _____
45) – 14 – 6 – 5 – 5 – 10   _____
46) + 2 + 4 + 4 + 5 + 6   _____
47) + 12 + 6 + 4 + 6 + 4 + 8   _____
48) – 13 – 7 – 6 – 8 – 12   _____
49) + 15 + 16 + 10 + 9 + 12 + 4   _____
50) – 11 – 17 – 5 – 18 – 6 – 22   _____

_____ %

Simplify using the mixed-sign rule.

See ASG, pp. 39–41

1) + 2 – 1 _____
2) + 4 – 3 _____
3) – 5 + 2 _____
4) – 4 + 6 _____
5) + 8 – 2 _____
6) – 4 + 2 _____
7) + 5 – 3 _____
8) – 7 + 8 _____
9) + 7 – 3 _____
10) + 4 – 2 _____
11) – 8 + 3 _____
12) + 7 – 6 _____
13) + 7 – 5 _____
14) – 9 + 6 _____
15) + 6 – 9 _____
16) – 8 + 2 _____
17) – 2 + 7 _____
18) – 3 + 9 _____
19) + 9 – 1 _____
20) + 9 – 8 _____
21) – 11 + 8 _____
22) + 3 – 35 _____
23) + 6 – 22 _____
24) + 4 – 14 _____
25) + 48 – 8 _____
26) – 4 + 17 _____
27) – 7 + 13 _____
28) + 6 – 15 _____
29) + 15 – 6 _____
30) – 27 + 9 _____
31) + 18 – 28 _____
32) – 16 + 23 _____
33) – 21 + 34 _____
34) + 15 – 45 _____
35) – 18 + 32 _____

36) – 42 + 52 _____
37) + 63 – 23 _____
38) – 72 + 36 _____
39) + 19 – 47 _____
40) + 86 – 41 _____
41) + 26 – 18 _____
42) – 12 + 43 _____
43) – 17 + 16 _____
44) + 29 – 14 _____
45) – 16 + 31 _____
46) + 62 – 41 _____
47) + 17 – 62 _____
48) + 43 – 39 _____
49) – 86 + 62 _____
50) + 97 – 72 _____
51) + 100 – 200 _____
52) – 151 + 153 _____
53) + 182 – 150 _____
54) – 260 + 180 _____
55) + 476 – 273 _____
56) + 815 – 453 _____
57) + 750 – 250 _____
58) – 681 + 412 _____
59) + 999 – 633 _____
60) + 873 – 384 _____
61) + 331 – 368 _____
62) – 823 + 134 _____
63) + 198 – 473 _____
64) + 183 – 496 _____
65) – 552 + 914 _____
66) + 959 – 267 _____
67) – 657 + 833 _____
68) – 551 + 951 _____
69) – 265 + 374 _____
70) + 597 – 899 _____

_____ %

First write S or M to show if you use the same-sign rule (S) or the mixed-sign rule (M). Then simplify.

See ASG, pp. 36–40

	Problem	S or M	Simplify
1)	– 3 – 7		
2)	+ 3 – 7		
3)	+ 3 + 7		
4)	– 3 + 7		
5)	– 8 + 5		
6)	+ 8 – 5		
7)	– 8 – 5		
8)	+ 8 + 5		
9)	– 6 + 2		
10)	+ 9 + 4		
11)	+ 13 – 6		
12)	+ 13 + 8		
13)	– 1 + 14		
14)	– 8 – 12		
15)	+ 4 + 17		
16)	+ 15 + 30		
17)	+ 13 – 23		
18)	– 10 + 18		
19)	– 21 + 18		
20)	+ 17 – 13		

_____ %

Simplify using the same- or mixed-sign rule.

See ASG, p. 42

1) + 4 – 3 + 2 _____
2) + 5 – 4 + 3 _____
3) – 6 – 4 + 5 _____
4) – 7 + 15 – 8 _____
5) + 8 + 4 – 10 _____
6) + 18 – 6 + 3 _____
7) + 11 – 22 – 33 _____
8) + 17 + 13 – 14 _____
9) – 26 – 13 + 19 _____
10) + 4 – 18 – 8 + 6 _____

11) + 4 + 18 + 8 + 6 _____
12) – 4 + 18 + 8 – 6 _____
13) – 21 – 14 – 55 + 10 _____
14) + 46 – 17 – 13 + 14 _____
15) + 81 – 25 – 36 + 10 _____
16) + 8 – 102 + 42 + 11 _____
17) – 273 + 61 – 9 + 186 _____
18) + 636 – 363 – 131 – 11 _____
19) + 512 – 256 + 128 + 64 _____
20) – 225 – 121 + 49 + 9 _____

_____ %

When solving equations, you often encounter the same- or mixed-sign rule in a vertical format. So expressions like $+3+5$ or $-4+7$ will appear as

$$\begin{array}{r} +\,3 \\ +\,5 \\ \hline \end{array} \quad \text{or} \quad \begin{array}{r} -\,4 \\ +\,7 \\ \hline \end{array}$$

NEW CONCEPT!

Don't let this vertical format throw you. Here's a chance to practice.

Combine the following terms using the same-sign rule.

_____ %

1)	2)	3)	4)	5)
$+\ 4$ $+\ 6$	$-\ 17$ $-\ 4$	$+\ 18$ $+\ 9$	$-\ 43$ $-\ 17$	$-\ 8$ $-\ 37$

Combine the following terms using the mixed-sign rule.

_____ %

1)	2)	3)	4)	5)
$+\ 2$ $-\ 7$	$-\ 12$ $+\ 18$	$+\ 62$ $-\ 45$	$-\ 48$ $+\ 39$	$-\ 27$ $+\ 55$

Combine the following terms using either the same- or mixed-sign rule.

1)	2)	3)	4)	5)
$+\ 13$ $+\ 24$	$-\ 18$ $+\ 21$	$+\ 25$ $-\ 21$	$-\ 16$ $-\ 15$	$-\ 25$ $+\ 36$

6)	7)	8)	9)	10)
$-\ 21$ $+\ 35$	$+\ 24$ $+\ 28$	$+\ 18$ $-\ 27$	$+\ 21$ $+\ 35$	$-\ 13$ $-\ 41$

11)	12)	13)	14)	15)
$-\ 37$ $+\ 57$	$-\ 11$ $-\ 45$	$+\ 17$ $-\ 62$	$+\ 42$ $-\ 18$	$-\ 13$ $-\ 36$

16)	17)	18)	19)	20)
$+\ 21$ $+\ 52$	$+\ 45$ $+\ 31$	$-\ 52$ $-\ 39$	$-\ 23$ $+\ 47$	$+\ 28$ $-\ 35$

21)	22)	23)	24)	25)
$-\ 46$ $+\ 51$	$+\ 45$ $+\ 28$	$-\ 23$ $-\ 56$	$+\ 32$ $-\ 55$	$+\ 62$ $+\ 89$

26)	27)	28)	29)	30)
$-\ 58$ $-\ 36$	$-\ 41$ $+\ 68$	$+\ 87$ $-\ 53$	$+\ 85$ $+\ 37$	$-\ 91$ $+\ 66$

_____ %

First show what happens after using the neighbor-sign rule. Then write S or M to show if you use the same- or mixed-sign rule. Then simplify.

See ASG, pp. 43–47

	Problem	After using neighbor-sign rule	S or M	Simplify
1)	– 3 + (– 2)			
2)	– 8 + + 5			
3)	+ 7 – – 4			
4)	– 9 – (+ 7)			
5)	+ 6 + – 7			
6)	+ 8 + + 4			
7)	– 7 – – 3			
8)	+ 2 – + 2			
9)	– 1 – (– 8)			
10)	– 4 + – 6			
11)	+ 12 + (+ 8)			
12)	– 7 + – 17			
13)	+ 24 – + 9			
14)	+ 4 – – 31			
15)	– 46 + – 8			
16)	+ 27 – (+ 35)			
17)	– 61 – – 45			
18)	– 86 + – 52			
19)	– 76 + + 63			
20)	+ 21 – (– 81)			
21)	– 126 + – 804			
22)	+ 312 – + 392			
23)	+ 181 – (– 406)			
24)	– 240 + – 376			
25)	+ 621 + + 412			

_____ %

Simplify.   See ASG, p. 48

1) $- 6 + (- 8) + 3$ _____

2) $+ 1 - 1 + -7$ _____

3) $- 4 - - 2 + 4 + - 3$ _____

4) $- 5 + 4 - - 1$ _____

5) $+ 9 - 8 + (- 5)$ _____

6) $- 8 - + 6 + 9 - - 1$ _____

7) $+ 7 - 2 - - 6$ _____

8) $+ 7 + (- 5) + 5$ _____

9) $+ 4 + (+ 1) - (+ 3) - 4$ _____

10) $- 6 + 8 + - 5 - + 1$ _____

11) $- 3 + - 12 + - 5 + + 17$ _____

12) $+ 21 - - 1 - + 43 + - 8 + - 8$ _____

13) $- 9 - + 24 - - 4 - + 52$ _____

14) $- 86 - (- 7) + (+ 41) - (- 1) - (+ 62)$ _____

15) $+ 5 + 18 + - 9 + + 61$ _____

16) $- 38 - + 9 - + 80 - - 2 + - 4$ _____

17) $+ 46 - - 61 - - 2 + - 14 - - 82$ _____

18) $+ 54 - (+ 72) + (- 86) - (+ 6) + (- 16)$ _____

19) $+ 5 + + 63 - + 42 + - 28 - + 81$ _____

20) $- 84 - - 3 + - 91 + + 30 + - 52$ _____

_____ %

Simplify using the multiplication rule.   See ASG, pp. 49–50

1) $(+ 3) \cdot (- 2)$ _____   6) $(- 8) \cdot (+ 3) \cdot (- 2)$ _____

2) $(- 6) \cdot (+ 4)$ _____   7) $(- 8) \cdot (- 14) \cdot (- 4)$ _____

3) $(+ 8) \cdot (+ 7)$ _____   8) $(- 18) \cdot (+ 3) \cdot (- 9)$ _____

4) $(+ 4) \cdot (- 13)$ _____   9) $(- 6) \cdot (+ 10) \cdot (+ 5)$ _____

5) $(- 16) \cdot (- 4)$ _____   10) $(+ 4) \cdot (- 1) \cdot (- 17)$ _____

_____ %

Simplify using the division rule.   See ASG, p. 51

1) $(+24)/(-3)$ _____
2) $(+18)/(+6)$ _____
3) $(-16)/(+4)$ _____
4) $(-20)/(-6)$ _____
5) $(+35)/(+7)$ _____

6) $(-46)/(-2)$ _____
7) $(+19)/(-4)$ _____
8) $(+63)/(+9)$ _____
9) $(+80)/(-10)$ _____
10) $(-99)/(+11)$ _____

_____ %

Tell which operation comes before which other one, then simplify.   See ASG, p. 59

1) $(25 - 16)^2$ _____
2) $(8 + 1) \cdot (4 \div 2)$ _____
3) $2^2 - 4^2$ _____
4) $(2 - 4)^2$ _____
5) $3^2 \cdot 4^2$ _____
6) $+ 3 - 4 - 9 + 2$ _____
7) $16/4 + 6$ _____
8) $(4 + 3) - (8 + 1)$ _____
9) $(8 \cdot 2) - 6^2$ _____
10) $2^2 + 6^2$ _____

_____ %

Don't simplify. Just tell which enclosure marks you'd work out first, second, and possibly third in the following problems.   See ASG, p. 60

1) $[(3 + 6) \div 5] \cdot 2$ _____
2) $\{3 + (4 + 6)^2\}$ _____
3) $([8 - \{4 + 6\}^2 \div 12] - 8)^2$ _____
4) $[8 + \{(26 - 8) \div 4\}] \div 2$ _____
5) $|(4 - 3)^2 - 86|$ _____
6) $16 + (8 + 3 \cdot [4 - 8]) \div 2$ _____
7) $|([16 - 32] \cdot 16) - 100|$ _____
8) $\{(|8 - 16| \cdot 8) - 50\} + 2$ _____
9) $[4 \cdot 3\{8 + |2 - 4|\} \div 62] + 4$ _____
10) $\{[(8 + 7)^2 - 100] \div 5\} + 20$ _____

_____ %

Use the order of operations to simplify the following problems. *See ASG, p. 62*

1) $4^2 + 8(3 \cdot 2)$ _____

2) $3 + [8 - (4 + 3)^2]$ _____

3) $2(4 + 3) + (-16)(4 - 6)$ _____

4) $\{15 - (3 \cdot 2)\} \div 3$ _____

5) $3^2 - (-1) + (-30 \div 2)$ _____

6) $7 + ([3 - 7] + 4^2) \div 2$ _____

7) $(-6) - (4 \cdot 3)(3 - 1) - 2^2$ _____

8) $(3 + 4)^2$ _____

9) $(3^2 + 4^2)$ _____

10) $5 - [(4 \cdot 5) \div 2]$ _____

11) $\{[(3 + 5) \div 2]^2 - (3 \cdot 2)\} \cdot (-2)$ _____

12) $[(4 \cdot 6) - (3 \cdot 2)] \div 2$ _____

13) $[3^2 - (2^2 \cdot 4)] + 7$ _____

14) $3 + \{(4 + 3) \cdot 6 - 2\}$ _____

15) $\{(8 - 3) \cdot 4 - [6(2 + 3) - 10]\} + 4$ _____

16) $(2)(3) + (3)(4) - (4)(5)$ _____

17) $[8 + (4)(5)] \div (2 - 6)$ _____

18) $(40 \cdot 2) \div [(12 \cdot 2) - 4]$ _____

19) $7 \cdot 8 \div 4 - 20$ _____

20) $15 \cdot 3 \div 5 + 12 \div 2$ _____

_____ %

Multiply and divide. *See ASG, p. 63*

1) $50 \div 5 \times 2$ _____

2) $50 \times 2 \div 5$ _____

3) $50 \div 5 \div 2$ _____

4) $50 \div (5 \times 2)$ _____

5) $50 \div 2 \times 5$ _____

6) $50 \times 5 \div 2$ _____

7) $50 \times (5 \div 2)$ _____

8) $6 \times 3 \div 2$ _____

9) $3 \div 2 \times 6$ _____

10) $2 \div 3 \times 6$ _____

11) $3 \times 2 \div 6$ _____

12) $4 \times 7 \div 2 \times 3$ _____

13) $4 \times 7 \times 3 \div 2$ _____

14) $3 \div 2 \times 4 \times 7$ _____

15) $4 \times 3 \div 2 \div 6$ _____

16) $4 \div 3 \times 2 \times 6$ _____

17) $4 \times 3 \div (2 \times 6)$ _____

18) $4 \div 2 \times 3 \div 6$ _____

19) $2 \times 3 \div 4 \times 6$ _____

20) $2 \times 3 \div (4 \times 6)$ _____

_____ %

Simplify.
See ASG, p. 64

1) $2 \cdot 3^2$ _____
2) $4 \cdot 2^2$ _____
3) $2 \cdot 4^2$ _____
4) $4 \cdot 3^2$ _____
5) $3 \cdot 4^2$ _____
6) $(2 \cdot 6)^2$ _____
7) $(5 \cdot 3)^2$ _____
8) $7 \cdot 2^2$ _____
9) $2 \cdot 7^2$ _____
10) $(5 \cdot 2)^2$ _____

1a) $(2 \cdot 3)^2$ _____
2a) $(4 \cdot 2)^2$ _____
3a) $(2 \cdot 4)^2$ _____
4a) $(4 \cdot 3)^2$ _____
5a) $(3 \cdot 4)^2$ _____
6a) $2 \cdot 6^2$ _____
7a) $5 \cdot 3^2$ _____
8a) $(7 \cdot 2)^2$ _____
9a) $(2 \cdot 7)^2$ _____
10a) $5 \cdot 2^2$ _____

_____ %

Simplify.
See ASG, p. 65

1) -2^2 _____
2) -3^2 _____
3) -4^2 _____
4) -5^2 _____
5) -6^2 _____
6) $(-7)^2$ _____
7) $(-8)^2$ _____
8) -9^2 _____
9) $(-10)^2$ _____
10) -11^2 _____

1a) $(-2)^2$ _____
2a) $(-3)^2$ _____
3a) $(-4)^2$ _____
4a) $(-5)^2$ _____
5a) $(-6)^2$ _____
6a) -7^2 _____
7a) -8^2 _____
8a) $(-9)^2$ _____
9a) -10^2 _____
10a) $(-11)^2$ _____

_____ %

Tell whether or not these terms are like terms.
See ASG, p. 67

1) $6,\ 3/5,\ -7/12$ _____
2) $mn,\ 3mp,\ 2np$ _____
3) $xyz,\ yzx,\ zxq$ _____
4) $1/4,\ 0.363,\ -4/3$ _____
5) $df^2e,\ 4def^2,\ 2dfe^2$ _____

6) $3a^2b,\ a^2b,\ 4ba^2$ _____
7) $2mcq,\ mq^2c,\ 2qmc$ _____
8) $a^2x^2m^2,\ 4m^2a^2x^2,\ \frac{1}{4}m^2x^2a^2$ _____
9) $0.25rq,\ qr,\ \frac{1}{5}rq$ _____
10) $ah^2m,\ m^2ha,\ a^2hm$ _____

_____ %

Add or subtract like terms.

See ASG, p. 68

1) 3m + 2m   _____
2) 2q – q   _____
3) 4rmx – 3rmx   _____
4) ab + ab + ab   _____
5) c^2d + c^2d _____

6) 2rm – mr   _____
7) z^2 + z^2 _____
8) $5t^2v$ – $3vt^2$ _____
9) 3aq – aq – 2aq _____
10) $4x^2z$ + zx^2 _____

_____ %

Make up funny names for like terms.

See ASG, p. 70

Example:

8b – 3b   *think:* _8 bananas – 3 bananas = 5 bananas_

So: _8b – 3b = 5b_

1)   4a + 2a   *think:* _____
   So: _____

2)   3x + 2x   *think:* _____
   So: _____

3)   6m – 2m   *think:* _____
   So: _____

4)   4r + r   *think:* _____
   So: _____

5)   5c – 2c   *think:* _____
   So: _____

6)   4y + y + y   *think:* _____
   So: _____

7)   2b – 2b   *think:* _____
   So: _____

8)   6f – 3f – 2f   *think:* _____
   So: _____

9) $2r^2$ + $3r^2$ *think:* _____
   So: _____

10) 4mn – 2mn   *think:* _____
   So: _____

_____ %

When solving equations, expressions that combine like terms often appear in a vertical format. For example, expressions like + 2x + 7x or − 3b + 8b can appear as:

$$+ 2x \atop + 7x$$ or $$- 3b \atop + 8b$$

NEW CONCEPT!

Just use the same- or mixed-sign rule. Here are some practice problems.

Combine the following terms using the same-sign rule.

1) + 3x
    + 7x

2) − 14y
    − 5y

3) + 8m
    + 18m

4) − 19a
    − 3a

5) − 13q
    − 15q

_____ %

Combine the following terms using the mixed-sign rule.

1) + 4n
    − 9n

2) − 16p
    + 7p

3) + 13c
    − 18c

4) − 11d
    + 24d

5) + 15r
    − 22r

_____ %

Combine the following terms using either the same- or mixed-sign rule.

1) + 11f
    + 8f

2) + 4x
    − 19x

3) − 15c
    + 11c

4) − 16h
    − 12h

5) + 18e
    − 23e

6) + 17d
    − 12d

7) + 8w
    + 13w

8) − 21x
    + 13x

9) + 10v
    + 7v

10) − 9b
    − 18b

11) + 16d
    − 25d

12) − 22a
    − 15a

13) − 13z
    + 28z

14) − 11m
    + 18m

15) − 8r
    − 24r

16) + 23u
    + 18u

17) + 6t
    + 17t

18) − 13q
    − 18q

19) + 4c
    − 19c

20) − 16m
    + 18m

21) + 13b
    − 24b

22) + 26s
    + 19s

23) − 18p
    − 19p

24) − 14k
    + 23k

25) + 21h
    + 25h

26) − 23n
    − 17n

27) + 19a
    − 28a

28) − 11j
    + 27j

29) + 25g
    + 17g

30) + 18y
    − 25y

_____ %

Simplify.

See ASG, p. 71

1) $mn + 2mn$ _____

2) $4mq - 7mq$ _____

3) $-6rx - 2rx$ _____

4) $-3bcx + 2bcx$ _____

5) $rx^2 + rx^2$ _____

6) $-dq^2 - 2dq^2$ _____

7) $3mp + - mp$ _____

8) $n^2c - + n^2c$ _____

9) $-fv + 3fv$ _____

10) $-gh - 2hg$ _____

11) $4pt + + 2pt$ _____

12) $3r^2nw - 2r^2nw$ _____

13) $xq - 5qx$ _____

14) $b^2c + b^2c + b^2c$ _____

15) $def - 3fed$ _____

16) $-3r^2nz + 5r^2nz$ _____

17) $abc + 3abc + - 4abc$ _____

18) $p^2 + 3.2p^2 - 1.1p^2$ _____

19) $-12r^2pq - + 16pqr^2$ _____

20) $-3bdf^2 - - 5df^2b$ _____

____ %

Simplify.

See ASG, p. 72

1) $x + y + 2x + y$ _____

2) $m - 1 - m + 3$ _____

3) $2q - 3q + 3 + 1$ _____

4) $5bc + - 2df - - 3df + bc$ _____

5) $-6xz + 6 - + 4 + 5xz$ _____

6) $hn - 2hn + bq - 2bq$ _____

7) $m - 4m + 2 + 3.2$ _____

8) $-y^2 + y + 3y^2 - 3y$ _____

9) $2cd^2 - 3f - - f + 6d^2c$ _____

10) $6xy + 5/6 - + 2xy + - 3/6$ _____

11) $6np - 4pr - 3pn + 2rp$ _____

12) $3n^2 + 4 - - 3 + - 3n^2 - 7$ _____

13) $8qh - + qt - 2qh - + 2qt$ _____

14) $5p^2 + 6p - 3p^2 - 2p^2$ _____

15) $ty - 2.25 + + 3ty - 1.75$ _____

16) $r^2 + pr + 3r^2 - + 3pr$ _____

17) $2n^2x + 3xn^2 + - 3 - - 7.3$ _____

18) $5xy - 2xy + yz - - 2yz + xy$ _____

19) $-3r^2 + mt + - 3mt + - 4r^2$ _____

20) $2r^2qb - + rqb + 3bqr + 3qbr^2$ _____

____ %

Simplify.   See ASG, p. 73

1) + (a + b) _____
2) + (a – b) _____
3) – (a + b) _____
4) – (a – b) _____
5) – (y + 6) _____
6) + (y – 6) _____
7) + (y + 6) _____
8) – (y – 6) _____
9) – (3 + g) _____
10) – (6 – m) _____

11) + (–3 + x) _____
12) – (n + p + 2) _____
13) + (p + r – 3) _____
14) – (a – b – c) _____
15) – (–2 + q) _____
16) + (m – n + p) _____
17) – (d + e – 6) _____
18) – (–x – y – z) _____
19) + (p – q – r) _____
20) – (–a – 4 + c) _____

_____ %

Simplify.   See ASG, p. 74

1) 8 + (a – 3) _____
2) 4 – (b + 3) _____
3) 6 – (3 – c) _____
4) 5 + (d – 2) _____
5) 2 + (e – 5) _____
6) 3 – (f + 3) _____
7) – 7 + (3 – g) _____
8) 4 – (6 + h) _____
9) 5 + (j – 6) _____
10) – 8 – (10 – k) _____
11) 2 + (–m – 2) _____
12) 7 – (–n – 8) _____
13) 7 + (p + 8) _____
14) – 3 – (q – 6) _____
15) – 5 + (r – 5) _____
16) 2 – (5 + s) _____
17) 6 + (t – 6) _____
18) – 9 + (–6 – u) _____
19) 7 – (v + 3) _____
20) – 1 – (w – 1) _____

_____ %

Determine the value.

See ASG, p. 78

1) $|4|$ _____
2) $|-4|$ _____
3) $|-2/3|$ _____
4) $|42|$ _____
5) $|-1.6|$ _____

6) $|7.25|$ _____
7) $|-7.25|$ _____
8) $|-5/6|$ _____
9) $|5/6|$ _____
10) $|-9|$ _____

_____%

Simplify.

See ASG, p. 79

1) $|1 + 3 - 6|$ _____
2) $|4 \cdot 5|$ _____
3) $|(-4)(5)|$ _____
4) $|3(2 - 6)|$ _____
5) $|36/6|$ _____
6) $|-36/6|$ _____
7) $|3 - (4 \cdot 3) + 7|$ _____
8) $|5 + (2 \cdot 3) - 11|$ _____
9) $|(3)(-2) - 6|$ _____
10) $|(-3)(4) - (3)(4)|$ _____

_____%

Simplify.

See ASG, p. 80

1) $2 + |3 - 8|$ _____
2) $6 - |4 + 3|$ _____
3) $2 \cdot |2 - 4|$ _____
4) $|(3)(-2)| - 3$ _____
5) $|(3)(-2) - 6| - 15$ _____
6) $|3 \cdot 4| \div 2$ _____
7) $|(3)(-4)| \div 2$ _____
8) $|(3)(-4)| \div (-2)$ _____
9) $|(2)(-5) - 5| - 5$ _____
10) $10 \div |7 + (3)(-4)|$ _____
11) $(-15) \div |3 \cdot 2 - 1|$ _____
12) $-4 - |(-9)(2) \div 3|$ _____
13) $8 + |(3)(-6) + 14|$ _____
14) $|8 - (3)(4)| - 4$ _____
15) $3 + |(5)(-2) + 1| - 16$ _____

_____%

Simplify.

See ASG, p. 81

1) $(-3) \cdot |3 - 5|$ _____

2) $|3 - 9|/2$ _____

3) $|6 - 2|^2$ _____

4) $-10/|6 - 11|$ _____

5) $(-5) \cdot |5 - 6|$ _____

6) $(-2) \cdot |3 - 8|^2$ _____

7) $|12 - 3|/3$ _____

8) $|8 - 2| \cdot |4 - 8|$ _____

9) $|4 - 8|^2 - 17$ _____

10) $|6 - 3|^2$ _____

11) $5 \cdot |7 - 9|$ _____

12) $-3 - |2 \cdot 5|$ _____

13) $|(-2)(6)|^2$ _____

14) $100/|(-5)(5)|$ _____

15) $(|-7| \cdot |4|)/(-2)$ _____

16) $12 \cdot |12 - 15|$ _____

17) $|14 - 6 \cdot 3| \cdot (-4)$ _____

18) $|-5|^2/5$ _____

19) $3^3/|4^2 - 5^2|$ _____

20) $|7 - 12| \cdot (7 - 12)$ _____

_____ %

Simplify.

See ASG, p. 82

1) $+ |-5|$ _____

2) $- |+8|$ _____

3) $- |-9|$ _____

4) $+ |+7|$ _____

5) $+ |-9|$ _____

6) $9 - |-2|$ _____

7) $- 8 + |-6|$ _____

8) $6 - |+5|$ _____

9) $5 - |-3|$ _____

10) $3 - |+5|$ _____

_____ %

Work out the values of the following exponential terms.

See ASG, p. 86

1) 3^2 _____
2) n^2 _____
3) n^3 _____
4) 2^3 _____
5) $(4x)^2$ _____

6) 3^3 _____
7) b^3 _____
8) 8^2 _____
9) $(pq)^2$ _____
10) $(1/4)^2$ _____

_____ %

Simplify. (Write each answer as a term to a power.)

See ASG, p. 89

1) $3^8 \cdot 3^2$ _____
2) $w^2 \cdot w^6$ _____
3) $4^m \cdot 4^n$ _____
4) $6^2 \cdot 6^4$ _____
5) $aardvark^2 \cdot aardvark^5$ _____
6) $p^3 \cdot p^6$ _____
7) $4^3 \cdot 4^8$ _____
8) $2^{hip} \cdot 2^{hop}$ _____
9) $r^2 \cdot r^{10}$ _____
10) $6^x \cdot 6^y$ _____

11) $10^4 \cdot 10^{10} \cdot 10^6$ _____
12) $a^6 \cdot a^9$ _____
13) $\triangle^9 \cdot \triangle^6$ _____
14) $c^8 \cdot c^7$ _____
15) $12^2 \cdot 12^8$ _____
16) $t^{2n} \cdot t^{3n}$ _____
17) $a^b \cdot a^c$ _____
18) $\diamond^3 \cdot \diamond^6$ _____
19) $87^{16} \cdot 87^{20}$ _____
20) $(xy)^w \cdot (xy)^z$ _____

_____ %

Simplify.

See ASG, p. 91

1) $\dfrac{3^{10}}{3^6}$ _____

2) $\dfrac{w^{10}}{w^6}$ _____

3) $\dfrac{5^6}{5^2}$ _____

4) $\dfrac{\bullet^9}{\bullet^4}$ _____

5) $\dfrac{8^a}{8^b}$ _____

6) $\dfrac{a^{10}}{a^2}$ _____

7) $\dfrac{tic^{tac}}{tic^{toe}}$ _____

8) $\dfrac{(p+q)^r}{(p+q)^s}$ _____

9) $\dfrac{\heartsuit^{12}}{\heartsuit^5}$ _____

10) $\dfrac{m^d}{m^d}$ _____

_____ %

22

When solving a problem like $(3x) \cdot (5x^2)$, first multiply the coefficients together, then multiply the variables together. Then string the two answers together. So to simplify $(3x) \cdot (5x^2)$, first multiply $3 \cdot 5 = 15$. Then multiply $x \cdot x^2 = x^3$. String the two answers together to get $15x^3$ as the final answer.

NEW CONCEPT!

1) $4y \cdot 2y$ _____

2) $6p^2 \cdot 7p$ _____

3) $2m^2 \cdot 3m^2$ _____

4) $5b^4 \cdot 5b^3$ _____

5) $4x^2 \cdot 8x^3$ _____

6) $12v \cdot v$ _____

7) $6t \cdot 2t^8$ _____

8) $3a^4 \cdot 4a^6$ _____

9) $9f \cdot 6$ _____

10) $10c^3 \cdot 5c^3$ _____

11) $5 \cdot 8w$ _____

12) $3e^2 \cdot 5e^2$ _____

13) $y \cdot 4y$ _____

14) $2p \cdot 3p \cdot 4p^2$ _____

15) $2x \cdot 3x^2 \cdot 5x^3$ _____

_____ %

When solving a problem like $12a^5/4a^3$, first divide the coefficients, then divide the variable terms, then put the two together. In this example, first divide 12 by 4 to get 3. Then divide a^5 by a^3 to get a^2. Put the two answers together to get the final answer, $3a^2$.

NEW CONCEPT!

1) $\dfrac{6m^2}{3m}$ _____

2) $\dfrac{9r^3}{3r}$ _____

3) $\dfrac{12p^4}{3p}$ _____

4) $\dfrac{15q^5}{3q}$ _____

5) $\dfrac{15m^{12}}{5m^4}$ _____

6) $\dfrac{10a}{5a}$ _____

7) $\dfrac{12e^3}{12e}$ _____

8) $\dfrac{7y}{7}$ _____

9) $\dfrac{3t^8}{2t^4}$ _____

10) $\dfrac{7x}{7x}$ _____

11) $\dfrac{18p^x}{3p^y}$ _____

12) $\dfrac{21d^{10}}{3d^2}$ _____

13) $\dfrac{6c^7}{3c^2}$ _____

14) $\dfrac{4x^{11}}{2x^5}$ _____

15) $\dfrac{8d^5}{2d^2}$ _____

_____ %

NAME _____   DATE _____

Simplify the following expressions.   See ASG, pp. 88 and 94

1) 3^1 _____
2) 3^0 _____
3) $(-10)^0$ _____
4) $(-10)^1$ _____
5) π^0 _____

6) π^1 _____
7) 7.865^0 _____
8) 12^1 _____
9) 162^1 _____
10) $(-14/3)^0$ _____

_____ %

Simplify the following expressions.   See ASG, p. 95

1) a^4b^0 _____
2) $6 - 4^0$ _____
3) $10 + w^0$ _____
4) $x^2y^4z^0$ _____
5) $x^0 + y^0 + a$ _____
6) mn^2p^0 _____

7) $m \cdot n^2 \cdot 4p^0$ _____
8) $r^2 - t^0$ _____
9) $\dfrac{a^3b^2c}{xy^0z^4}$ _____
10) $\dfrac{6 - a^0}{8 + a^0}$ _____

_____ %

Arrange the terms in descending order.   See ASG, p. 97

1) $-3 + y$ _____
2) $2y + y^2 - 6$ _____
3) $-m + 3 - m^2$ _____
4) $3b^2 + 2b^3 - 4 - 3b$ _____
5) $13 + n^2$ _____
6) $-c + 3 + 2c^2$ _____
7) $p^2 - 3p^3 + 9 - 2p^4 + 6p$ _____
8) $-3x + x^5 + 7$ _____
9) $9a - 5 + a^3 - 2a^2$ _____
10) $3e^2 - 2e + 5$ _____
11) $r^2 - 3r^3 + 4 - r + 8r^4$ _____
12) $2t^2 + 5 - t + 12t^3$ _____
13) $-5q - 3q^2 + 5$ _____
14) $3w^4 - 4w^3 + 6 - 2w^2 + 8w^5 - w$ _____
15) $5 + s - s^2 - s^3$ _____

_____ %

24

NAME _____ DATE _____

Rewrite the following terms using only positive exponents. See ASG, p. 98

1) x^{-2} _____ 6) 7^{-n} _____
2) b^{-4} _____ 7) $12^{-earring}$ _____
3) c^{-8} _____ 8) y^{-x} _____
4) $\diamond^{-5}$ _____ 9) cat^{-dog} _____
5) 9^{-2} _____ 10) 8^{-m} _____

_____ %

Rewrite the following terms using only positive exponents. See ASG, p. 100

1) $\dfrac{1}{2^{-7}}$ _____ 6) $\dfrac{1}{r^{-6}}$ _____
2) $\dfrac{1}{p^{-6}}$ _____ 7) $\dfrac{1}{8^{-c}}$ _____
3) $\dfrac{1}{3^{-x}}$ _____ 8) $\dfrac{1}{pizza^{-slice}}$ _____
4) $\dfrac{1}{\oplus^{-w}}$ _____ 9) $\dfrac{1}{\diamond^{-3}}$ _____
5) $\dfrac{1}{ski^{-snowboard}}$ _____ 10) $\dfrac{1}{7^{-1}}$ _____

_____ %

Rewrite the following terms using only positive exponents. See ASG, p. 102

1) $3x^{-2}y^{-3}$ _____
2) x^3y^{-2} _____
3) $\dfrac{2m^2n^{-4}}{5p^4r^{-3}}$ _____
4) $\dfrac{7}{a^{-2}b^{-3}c^{-5}}$ _____
5) $\dfrac{d^{-2}}{e^{-3}}$ _____
6) $r^2f^{-3}x^{-5}j^8$ _____
7) $6p^2r^{-2}$ _____
8) $\dfrac{n^2x^3p^{-4}}{6^{-2}m^2r^{-2}}$ _____
9) $\dfrac{3^{-2}xy^2}{5^{-2}m^3n^{-2}}$ _____
10) $\dfrac{a^{-n}b^{-m}c^{-p}}{d^{-x}e^{-y}f^{-z}}$ _____

_____ %

Simplify, keeping all exponents positive.   See ASG, p. 103

1) $\dfrac{2^7}{2^3}$ _____

2) $\dfrac{x^{12}}{x^5}$ _____

3) $\dfrac{4^2}{4^5}$ _____

4) $\dfrac{clone^6}{clone^{11}}$ _____

5) $\dfrac{m^3}{m^{-5}}$ _____

6) $\dfrac{z^{15}}{z^2}$ _____

7) $\dfrac{10^{-6}}{10^2}$ _____

8) $\dfrac{lemur^{-8}}{lemur^{-11}}$ _____

9) $\dfrac{r^{-2}}{r^{-1}}$ _____

10) $\dfrac{n^6}{n^{13}}$ _____

_____ %

Simplify, keeping all exponents positive.   See ASG, p. 104

1) $\dfrac{r^2 r^{-2}}{r^3 r^4 r^2}$ _____

2) $\dfrac{m^{-3} m^4}{m^{-6} m^2}$ _____

3) $\dfrac{3^{-2} \cdot 3^{-3} \cdot 3^{-4}}{3^4 \cdot 3^5 \cdot 3^6}$ _____

4) $\dfrac{x^{-6} x^2}{x^{-8} x^3}$ _____

5) $\dfrac{eel^{-4} \cdot eel^2}{eel^{-11} \cdot eel^{-4}}$ _____

6) $\dfrac{c^3 c^8}{c^{-5} c^{-4}}$ _____

7) $\dfrac{z^{-2} z^{-4} z^1}{z^{-3} z^{-5} z^6}$ _____

8) $\dfrac{pony^{-8} \cdot pony^3}{pony^{12} \cdot pony^{-6}}$ _____

9) $\dfrac{6^{10} \cdot 6^{-17} \cdot 6^4}{6^{-6} \cdot 6^{-2}}$ _____

10) $\dfrac{v^{-3} v^2}{v^{11} v^{-13} v^2}$ _____

_____ %

Simplify, keeping all exponents positive.   See ASG, p. 105

1) $\dfrac{a^2 b^{-4}}{b^{-3} a^{-4}}$ _____

2) $\dfrac{3^{-3} r^4}{r^{-2} 3^{-2}}$ _____

3) $\dfrac{4^{-4} w^6}{w^2 w^{-4} 4^{-5}}$ _____

4) $\dfrac{t^5 v^{-3} v^4}{v^{-5} t^7}$ _____

5) $\dfrac{8^{12} n^{-3} 8^{-4}}{n^4 8^{10}}$ _____

6) $\dfrac{c^8 e^5 e^{-3}}{c^6 e^2 c^2}$ _____

7) $\dfrac{d^{-7} 5^{-3}}{5^2 d^{-5} d^{-9} 5^{-8}}$ _____

8) $\dfrac{9^{-5} z^2 z^{-8} 9^{12}}{z^5 9^9}$ _____

9) $\dfrac{k^{17} u^{12} u^{-4}}{k^9 k^{13} u^2}$ _____

10) $\dfrac{s^{15} 7^{-13} 7^0 s^{-18}}{7^6 7^{-20} s^{-3}}$ _____

_____ %

Use the exponent-to-exponent rule to simplify these terms.   See ASG, p. 106

1) $(3^2)^4$ _____
2) $(a^3)^5$ _____
3) $(c^x)^y$ _____
4) $(4^{-3})^{-2}$ _____
5) $(llama^{-4})^{-4}$ _____
6) $(k^4)^{-2}$ _____
7) $(\odot^6)^5$ _____
8) $(p^x)^{-z}$ _____
9) $(gum^6)^6$ _____
10) $(n^{-4})^{-6}$ _____

11) $(6^{-2})^{-5}$ _____
12) $(12^6)^{-3}$ _____
13) $(\diamond^c)^f$ _____
14) $(3^3)^9$ _____
15) $(p^r)^4$ _____
16) $(8^{-8})^6$ _____
17) $(v^{10})^2$ _____
18) $(\star^v)^{-w}$ _____
19) $(e^4)^{-7}$ _____
20) $(bug^{-3})^d$ _____

_____ %

Simplify these expressions. Use only positive exponents.   See ASG, p. 108

1) $e^3(e^4)^2e^{-2}$ _____

2) $2^3p^0(p^3)^3$ _____

3) $\dfrac{x^{-3}(x^3)^2}{(x^4)^2x^{-10}}$ _____

4) $(r^3)^4(r^{-2})^3(-2)^2$ _____

5) $\dfrac{(b^{-2})^{-5}b^0b^6}{b^7b^{-2}(b^{-4})^{-4}}$ _____

6) $(4^{-2})^{-1}(z^2)^{-4}(z^{-5})^2$ _____

7) $(5^1)^{-1}t^{-3}(t^3)^4$ _____

8) $\dfrac{(k^{-6})^3k^5(k^3)^{-2}}{k^7(k^4)^6k^{-12}}$ _____

9) $\dfrac{v^9v^6(v^{-3})^3}{v^3(v^2)^{-4}v}$ _____

10) $\dfrac{(3^4)^2r^{-3}}{(3^2)^3(r^2)^6(r^3)^0}$ _____

11) $(w^{-5})^{-3}w^{-10}(w^{-2})^2$ _____

12) $\dfrac{c^4c^{17}(c^{-4})^4}{(c^5)^{-6}c^{14}}$ _____

13) $\dfrac{(4^{-3})^5n^4}{n^3(n^4)^{-2}(4^2)^{-6}}$ _____

14) $(3^{-2})^{-1}(y^{-3})^{-6}y^{-13}$ _____

15) $(d^{-3})^2d^8(d^4)^{-2}d^6$ _____

16) $a^4(a^2)^{-2}(5^{-1})^3$ _____

17) $\dfrac{(6^{-3})^2f^5}{(6^{-2})^2(f^{-3})^4}$ _____

18) $(s^2)^6(s^4)^{-4}s^{-3}$ _____

19) $\dfrac{(8^3)^7q^6(q^{-2})^8}{(q^2)^{-4}(8^{-4})^{-5}}$ _____

20) $(u^{13})^2(4^2)^{-1}(u^{-2})^{10}$ _____

_____ %

Simplify. Just use the product-to-exponent rule.   See ASG, p. 109

1) $(3 \cdot 5)^2$ _____

2) $(x \cdot y)^4$ _____

3) $(4 \cdot 7)^{-p}$ _____

4) $(a \cdot b)^x$ _____

5) $(tooth \cdot eye)^4$ _____

6) $(6 \cdot 3)^{-d}$ _____

7) $(2 \cdot 4 \cdot 5)^3$ _____

8) $(\triangle \cdot \square)^z$ _____

9) $(p \cdot q)^{-2}$ _____

10) $(c \cdot e)^y$ _____

_____ %

To simplify a term like $(3x)^2$, first apply the exponent to the coefficient, 3, to get 3^2 or 9. Then apply the exponent to the variable to get x^2. Then string the answers together to get $9x^2$.

NEW CONCEPT!

1) $(5y)^2$ _____

2) $(2z)^3$ _____

3) $(-3a)^2$ _____

4) $(4b)^3$ _____

5) $(3n)^2$ _____

6) $(-2d)^3$ _____

7) $(6c)^2$ _____

8) $(4h)^2$ _____

9) $(5e)^3$ _____

10) $(-7f)^2$ _____

11) $(8g)^2$ _____

12) $(-2b)^3$ _____

13) $(6p)^3$ _____

14) $(2r)^3$ _____

15) $(-4t)^2$ _____

16) $(3a)^4$ _____

17) $(7k)^2$ _____

18) $(-6m)^3$ _____

19) $(2z)^4$ _____

20) $(4j)^3$ _____

21) $(3w)^3$ _____

22) $(-6x)^2$ _____

23) $(7y)^3$ _____

24) $(4p)^4$ _____

25) $(-9n)^3$ _____

26) $(3q)^3$ _____

27) $(-4u)^3$ _____

28) $(-8s)^3$ _____

29) $(2v)^3$ _____

30) $(10x)^3$ _____

_____ %

Simplify, keeping all exponents positive.   See ASG, p. 110

1) $a^2(ba)^{-2}b$ _____

2) $7^{-2}e^{-3}(ce)^4$ _____

3) $\dfrac{w^2v(wv)^{-2}}{v^{-3}w^5(vw)^2}$ _____

4) $(pq)^3p^{-2}(pq)^{-2}q^4$ _____

5) $\dfrac{3^{-2}(rn)^4r^{-6}}{r^{-2}(3^{-1})n^{-2}}$ _____

6) $\dfrac{(3z)^{-2}z^8t}{t^3(3z^2)^{-4}z^6}$ _____

7) $9^{-2}y^{15}(xy)^{-3}(x^2y^2)^{-4}$ _____

8) $k^{-3}(yk)^4k^{-2}y^8$ _____

9) $\dfrac{a^2(ac)^5c^2}{c^{-2}(ac)^{-2}}$ _____

10) $(6m)^3d^2m^0(6m^2)^{-1}m^4$ _____

_____ %

Simplify these terms using the quotient-to-exponent rule.   See ASG, p. 111

1) $\left(\dfrac{m}{n}\right)^6$ _____

2) $\left(\dfrac{2}{5}\right)^3$ _____

3) $\left(\dfrac{\triangle}{\square}\right)^x$ _____

4) $\left(\dfrac{t}{w}\right)^c$ _____

5) $\left(\dfrac{3}{7}\right)^{-2}$ _____

6) $\left(\dfrac{2}{9}\right)^3$ _____

7) $\left(\dfrac{x}{y}\right)^{-3}$ _____

8) $\left(\dfrac{r}{c}\right)^{-p}$ _____

9) $\left(\dfrac{\bigstar}{\square}\right)^{\triangle}$ _____

10) $\left(\dfrac{3}{10}\right)^{-4}$ _____

_____ %

Simplify, keeping all exponents positive.   See ASG, p. 112

1) $\left(\dfrac{r}{m}\right)^4 \cdot \dfrac{m^2}{r^3}$ _____

2) $\dfrac{c^2b^{-3}}{b^2c^3} \cdot \left(\dfrac{b}{c}\right)^4$ _____

3) $\dfrac{3^2t^2}{3^4w^2} \cdot \left(\dfrac{t}{w}\right)^5$ _____

4) $\left(\dfrac{a}{c}\right)^{-3} \cdot \left(\dfrac{a}{c}\right)^5$ _____

5) $\dfrac{r^2}{e^{-6}} \cdot \left(\dfrac{2^2e^2}{2^3r^{-2}}\right)^{-1}$ _____

6) $\left(\dfrac{v}{n}\right)^{-3} \cdot \left(\dfrac{n}{v}\right)^{-6}$ _____

7) $\left(\dfrac{5^2}{5^3}\right)^{-3} \cdot \dfrac{dr^2}{d^3r}$ _____

8) $\dfrac{b^2}{c^5} \cdot \left(\dfrac{c}{b}\right)^{-3}$ _____

9) $\left(\dfrac{7^3}{7^4}\right) \cdot \dfrac{m^2n^{-3}}{n^{-5}m^{-6}}$ _____

10) $\left(\dfrac{2}{5}\right)^{-2} \cdot \dfrac{2^3 \cdot 5^2}{2^4 \cdot 5^6}$ _____

_____ %

Find the square roots.

See ASG, p. 116

1) $\sqrt{16}$ _____
2) $\sqrt{25}$ _____
3) $\sqrt{4}$ _____
4) $\sqrt{64}$ _____
5) $\sqrt{49}$ _____

6) $\sqrt{100}$ _____
7) $\sqrt{81}$ _____
8) $\sqrt{169}$ _____
9) $\sqrt{121}$ _____
10) $\sqrt{196}$ _____

_____ %

Find the value.

See ASG, p. 119

1) $\sqrt{25} \cdot \sqrt{25}$ _____
2) $\sqrt{12a} \cdot \sqrt{12a}$ _____
3) $\sqrt{7mn^2} \cdot \sqrt{7mn^2}$ _____
4) $\sqrt{w} \cdot \sqrt{w}$ _____
5) $\sqrt{\dfrac{1}{4}} \cdot \sqrt{\dfrac{1}{4}}$ _____

6) $\sqrt{c} \cdot \sqrt{c}$ _____
7) $\sqrt{19} \cdot \sqrt{19}$ _____
8) $\sqrt{36xy} \cdot \sqrt{36xy}$ _____
9) $\sqrt{salami} \cdot \sqrt{salami}$ _____
10) $\sqrt{16p^2q^2} \cdot \sqrt{16p^2q^2}$ _____

_____ %

Find the value.

See ASG, p. 120

1) $(\sqrt{18})^2$ _____
2) $(\sqrt{m})^2$ _____
3) $(\sqrt{rt})^2$ _____
4) $(\sqrt{1/8})^2$ _____
5) $(\sqrt{\smiley})^2$ _____

6) $(\sqrt{q})^2$ _____
7) $(\sqrt{8w^2})^2$ _____
8) $(\sqrt{mnp})^2$ _____
9) $(\sqrt{100x^2y})^2$ _____
10) $(\sqrt{magic})^2$ _____

_____ %

Find the perfect squares of the following terms.

See ASG, p. 123

1) 13 _____
2) y _____
3) 31 _____
4) 15 _____
5) r^2 _____

6) 1/5 _____
7) 12p _____
8) 18 _____
9) 111 _____
10) 10xy _____

_____ %

Combine the radicals.

See ASG, pp. 124–125

1) $3\sqrt{8} - + 5\sqrt{8}$ _____
2) $2\sqrt{7} - 8\sqrt{7}$ _____
3) $\sqrt{4} + 9\sqrt{4}$ _____
4) $6\sqrt{2} - - 7\sqrt{2}$ _____
5) $-4\sqrt{12} - 9\sqrt{12}$ _____

6) $-11\sqrt{u} + + 2\sqrt{u}$ _____
7) $15\sqrt{v} - 6\sqrt{v}$ _____
8) $-15\sqrt{a} - 6\sqrt{a}$ _____
9) $-13\sqrt{t} + - 3\sqrt{t}$ _____
10) $9\sqrt{x} + 8\sqrt{x}$ _____

_____ %

Combine using the radical product rule.

See ASG, p. 126

1) $\sqrt{2} \cdot \sqrt{5}$ _____
2) $\sqrt{3} \cdot \sqrt{7}$ _____
3) $\sqrt{a} \cdot \sqrt{c}$ _____
4) $\sqrt{d} \cdot \sqrt{x}$ _____
5) $\sqrt{6} \cdot \sqrt{y}$ _____

6) $\sqrt{a} \cdot \sqrt{13}$ _____
7) $\sqrt{frog} \cdot \sqrt{toad}$ _____
8) $\sqrt{rain} \cdot \sqrt{cloud}$ _____
9) $\sqrt{☆} \cdot \sqrt{□}$ _____
10) $\sqrt{△} \cdot \sqrt{☺}$ _____

_____ %

Use the radical product rule.

See ASG, p. 127

1) $\sqrt{3} \cdot \sqrt{12}$ _____
2) $\sqrt{2} \cdot \sqrt{8}$ _____
3) $\sqrt{16} \cdot \sqrt{4}$ _____
4) $\sqrt{6} \cdot \sqrt{24}$ _____
5) $\sqrt{18} \cdot \sqrt{8}$ _____
6) $\sqrt{7} \cdot \sqrt{28}$ _____
7) $\sqrt{a} \cdot \sqrt{a}$ _____
8) $\sqrt{m} \cdot \sqrt{m}$ _____
9) $\sqrt{3x} \cdot \sqrt{27x}$ _____
10) $\sqrt{4y} \cdot \sqrt{49y}$ _____

11) $\sqrt{9x} \cdot \sqrt{x}$ _____
12) $\sqrt{25c} \cdot \sqrt{4c}$ _____
13) $\sqrt{11e} \cdot \sqrt{11e}$ _____
14) $\sqrt{2k} \cdot \sqrt{18k}$ _____
15) $\sqrt{72p} \cdot \sqrt{2p}$ _____
16) $\sqrt{7w} \cdot \sqrt{7w}$ _____
17) $\sqrt{3z} \cdot \sqrt{3z} \cdot \sqrt{9}$ _____
18) $\sqrt{2} \cdot \sqrt{5u} \cdot \sqrt{10u}$ _____
19) $\sqrt{2} \cdot \sqrt{4n} \cdot \sqrt{8n}$ _____
20) $\sqrt{2r} \cdot \sqrt{7r} \cdot \sqrt{14}$ _____

_____ %

Split the squares.

See ASG, p. 128

1) $\sqrt{8 \cdot 5}$ _____
2) $\sqrt{11 \cdot 7}$ _____
3) $\sqrt{m \cdot p}$ _____
4) $\sqrt{x \cdot y}$ _____
5) $\sqrt{15 \cdot r}$ _____

6) $\sqrt{c^2 \cdot 16}$ _____
7) $\sqrt{red \cdot blue}$ _____
8) $\sqrt{foot \cdot hand}$ _____
9) $\sqrt{☆ \cdot ☉}$ _____
10) $\sqrt{☹ \cdot △}$ _____

_____ %

Simplify these terms by splitting the squares.

See ASG, p. 129

1) $\sqrt{8}$ _____

2) $\sqrt{12}$ _____

3) $\sqrt{18}$ _____

4) $\sqrt{20}$ _____

5) $\sqrt{32}$ _____

6) $\sqrt{45}$ _____

7) $\sqrt{50}$ _____

8) $\sqrt{52}$ _____

9) $\sqrt{60}$ _____

10) $\sqrt{63}$ _____

11) $\sqrt{72}$ _____

12) $\sqrt{75}$ _____

13) $\sqrt{80}$ _____

14) $\sqrt{90}$ _____

15) $\sqrt{96}$ _____

16) $\sqrt{98}$ _____

17) $\sqrt{128}$ _____

18) $\sqrt{135}$ _____

19) $\sqrt{136}$ _____

20) $\sqrt{200}$ _____

21) $\sqrt{144b^2}$ _____

22) $\sqrt{81m^2s^2}$ _____

23) $\sqrt{64q^2}$ _____

24) $\sqrt{121a^2}$ _____

25) $\sqrt{36x^2}$ _____

26) $\sqrt{9y^2k^2}$ _____

27) $\sqrt{169w^2}$ _____

28) $\sqrt{100e^2f^2}$ _____

29) $\sqrt{196n^2t^2}$ _____

30) $\sqrt{49r^2}$ _____

31) $\sqrt{32w^2}$ _____

32) $\sqrt{12g^2}$ _____

33) $\sqrt{80v^2}$ _____

34) $\sqrt{45r^2p^2}$ _____

35) $\sqrt{75k^2q^2}$ _____

36) $\sqrt{63b^2c}$ _____

37) $\sqrt{18xy^2}$ _____

38) $\sqrt{96u}$ _____

39) $\sqrt{64r}$ _____

40) $\sqrt{81s^2}$ _____

41) $\sqrt{a^2b^2x}$ _____

42) $\sqrt{mp^2}$ _____

43) $\sqrt{36xy^2}$ _____

44) $\sqrt{w^2td^2}$ _____

45) $\sqrt{81ab^2c^2}$ _____

46) $\sqrt{8w^2z^2}$ _____

47) $\sqrt{20e^2m^2}$ _____

48) $\sqrt{75p^2r^2q}$ _____

49) $\sqrt{64t^2a^2}$ _____

50) $\sqrt{216n^2s^2tv}$ _____

_____ %

True or false?

See ASG, p. 130

1) $\sqrt{72} = \sqrt{9} \cdot \sqrt{8}$ _____

2) $\sqrt{9 \cdot 10} = \sqrt{9} + \sqrt{10}$ _____

3) $\sqrt{13 - 5} = \sqrt{13} - \sqrt{5}$ _____

4) $\sqrt{18bx} = \sqrt{18} \cdot \sqrt{b} \cdot \sqrt{x}$ _____

5) $\sqrt{100 + 64} = \sqrt{100} + \sqrt{64}$ _____

6) $\sqrt{m + x} = \sqrt{m} + \sqrt{x}$ _____

7) $\sqrt{8 \cdot 12} = \sqrt{8} \cdot \sqrt{12}$ _____

8) $\sqrt{30} = \sqrt{5} \cdot \sqrt{6}$ _____

9) $\sqrt{44} = \sqrt{22} + \sqrt{22}$ _____

10) $\sqrt{10 \cdot 10} = \sqrt{10} \cdot \sqrt{10}$ _____

_____ %

Simplify.

See ASG, p. 131

1) $\sqrt{8^2}$ _____

2) $\sqrt{15^2}$ _____

3) $\sqrt{b^2}$ _____

4) $\sqrt{w^2}$ _____

5) $\sqrt{(4m)^2}$ _____

6) $\sqrt{(13a)^2}$ _____

7) $\sqrt{(hat)^2}$ _____

8) $\sqrt{(glove)^2}$ _____

9) $\sqrt{\square^2}$ _____

10) $\sqrt{\diamondsuit^2}$ _____

_____ %

Use the complex product radical rule to simplify these terms.

See ASG, p. 132

1) $3\sqrt{2} \cdot 4\sqrt{3}$ _____

2) $5\sqrt{5} \cdot 7\sqrt{3}$ _____

3) $a\sqrt{x} \cdot b\sqrt{y}$ _____

4) $m\sqrt{w} \cdot u\sqrt{v}$ _____

5) $8\sqrt{c} \cdot 3\sqrt{e}$ _____

6) $k\sqrt{5} \cdot n\sqrt{8}$ _____

7) $3\sqrt{tic} \cdot 6\sqrt{tac}$ _____

8) $7\sqrt{hot} \cdot 8\sqrt{cold}$ _____

9) $3\sqrt{\diamond} \cdot 4\sqrt{\triangledown}$ _____

10) $8\sqrt{\square} \cdot 6\sqrt{\triangle}$ _____

_____ %

Simplify these terms using the radical product shortcut.

See ASG, p. 133

1) $(4\sqrt{2})^2$ _____

2) $(6\sqrt{3})^2$ _____

3) $(7\sqrt{5})^2$ _____

4) $(3\sqrt{6})^2$ _____

5) $(y\sqrt{a})^2$ _____

6) $(b\sqrt{x})^2$ _____

7) $(5\sqrt{c})^2$ _____

8) $(6\sqrt{w})^2$ _____

9) $(v\sqrt{5})^2$ _____

10) $(p\sqrt{10})^2$ _____

_____ %

Use the radical quotient rule to simplify these terms.

See ASG, p. 134

1) $\dfrac{\sqrt{18}}{\sqrt{6}}$ _____

2) $\dfrac{\sqrt{a}}{\sqrt{c}}$ _____

3) $\dfrac{\sqrt{6m}}{\sqrt{8n}}$ _____

4) $\dfrac{\sqrt{arm}}{\sqrt{leg}}$ _____

_____ %

Simplify the following terms using the radical quotient rule.   See ASG, p. 135

1) $\dfrac{\sqrt{80}}{\sqrt{5}}$ _____

2) $\dfrac{\sqrt{54}}{\sqrt{6}}$ _____

3) $\dfrac{\sqrt{180}}{\sqrt{5}}$ _____

4) $\dfrac{\sqrt{28}}{\sqrt{7}}$ _____

5) $\dfrac{\sqrt{x^7}}{\sqrt{x^5}}$ _____

6) $\dfrac{\sqrt{m^7}}{\sqrt{m^3}}$ _____

7) $\dfrac{\sqrt{36a^3}}{\sqrt{4a}}$ _____

8) $\dfrac{\sqrt{320w^6}}{\sqrt{5w^2}}$ _____

_____ %

Split these radicals using the reverse radical quotient rule.   See ASG, p. 136

1) $\sqrt{\dfrac{8}{15}}$ _____

2) $\sqrt{\dfrac{m}{n}}$ _____

3) $\sqrt{\dfrac{mind}{matter}}$ _____

4) $\sqrt{\dfrac{\odot}{\bigstar}}$ _____

_____ %

Use the reverse radical quotient rule to simplify these terms.   See ASG, p. 137

1) $\sqrt{\dfrac{9}{25}}$ _____

2) $\sqrt{\dfrac{25}{36}}$ _____

3) $\sqrt{\dfrac{81}{100}}$ _____

4) $\sqrt{\dfrac{121}{196}}$ _____

5) $\sqrt{\dfrac{m^2}{y^2}}$ _____

6) $\sqrt{\dfrac{x}{16}}$ _____

7) $\sqrt{\dfrac{r^2}{15}}$ _____

8) $\sqrt{\dfrac{c^2}{144}}$ _____

_____ %

Simplify these terms using the complex radical quotient rule.   See ASG, p. 138

1) $\dfrac{3\sqrt{5}}{7\sqrt{9}}$ _____

2) $\dfrac{2\sqrt{7}}{13\sqrt{10}}$ _____

3) $\dfrac{a\sqrt{d}}{c\sqrt{q}}$ _____

4) $\dfrac{m\sqrt{x}}{n\sqrt{y}}$ _____

5) $\dfrac{2\sqrt{c}}{6\sqrt{r}}$ _____

6) $\dfrac{z\sqrt{15}}{f\sqrt{7}}$ _____

7) $\dfrac{6\sqrt{man}}{10\sqrt{board}}$ _____

8) $\dfrac{sip\sqrt{gulp}}{cup\sqrt{glass}}$ _____

9) $\dfrac{\triangle\sqrt{\star}}{\square\sqrt{\odot}}$ _____

10) $\dfrac{\nabla\sqrt{\diamond}}{\smiley\sqrt{\blacklozenge}}$ _____

_____ %

Simplify these terms by rationalizing the denominators.   See ASG, p. 139

1) $\dfrac{\sqrt{2}}{\sqrt{5}}$ _____

2) $\dfrac{\sqrt{5}}{\sqrt{6}}$ _____

3) $\dfrac{\sqrt{3}}{\sqrt{8}}$ _____

4) $\dfrac{5}{\sqrt{2}}$ _____

5) $\dfrac{9}{\sqrt{5}}$ _____

6) $\dfrac{4}{\sqrt{7}}$ _____

7) $\dfrac{a}{\sqrt{12}}$ _____

8) $\dfrac{m}{\sqrt{8}}$ _____

9) $\dfrac{r}{\sqrt{15}}$ _____

10) $\dfrac{\sqrt{c}}{\sqrt{11}}$ _____

11) $\dfrac{\sqrt{e}}{\sqrt{5}}$ _____

12) $\dfrac{\sqrt{x}}{\sqrt{18}}$ _____

13) $\dfrac{10}{\sqrt{5}}$ _____

14) $\dfrac{y}{\sqrt{19}}$ _____

15) $\dfrac{\sqrt{2}}{\sqrt{8}}$ _____

16) $\dfrac{\sqrt{12}}{\sqrt{3}}$ _____

17) $\dfrac{\sqrt{n}}{\sqrt{14}}$ _____

18) $\dfrac{12}{\sqrt{5}}$ _____

19) $\dfrac{t}{\sqrt{22}}$ _____

20) $\dfrac{\sqrt{13}}{\sqrt{3}}$ _____

_____ %

Are these terms in their original or factored forms?   See ASG, p. 142

1) 15 _____
2) $3x^2$ _____
3) $4 \cdot 5$ _____
4) $8 \cdot (p - 4)$ _____

5) 16xyz _____
6) $7r \cdot 3s$ _____
7) $4m^2n$ _____
8) $4p \cdot (t + 7)$ _____

_____ %

Identify the coefficient.   See ASG, pp. 143–144

1) 3mn _____
2) wv^2 _____
3) $(2/7)pqr$ _____
4) $- b^2c^2$ _____

5) $- 4x^2$ _____
6) x^2y _____
7) $- efg$ _____
8) 1.63k _____

_____ %

Tell whether these are monomials, binomials, or trinomials.   See ASG, p. 146

1) $- 4p^2$ _____
2) $m^6 + 3m^2$ _____
3) $- 3x^2 - x + 2$ _____
4) $2y + 3$ _____
5) $6.3a^2 - 1.2a$ _____

6) mp _____
7) $b^2 + 16b + 4$ _____
8) $- 6/13$ _____
9) $c^6 + 5c^4 - 4c^2$ _____
10) $2 + 3w$ _____

_____ %

List all the factors of these numbers.   See ASG, p. 148

1) 4 _____
2) 6 _____
3) 10 _____
4) 12 _____
5) 20 _____
6) 21 _____
7) 25 _____
8) 28 _____
9) 36 _____
10) 40 _____

11) 45 _____
12) 60 _____
13) 75 _____
14) 85 _____
15) 96 _____
16) 100 _____
17) 121 _____
18) 125 _____
19) 144 _____
20) 200 _____

_____ %

List the primary factors of these monomials.

See ASG, p. 149

1) $12p^2$ _____

2) $8xyz$ _____

3) $15b^2c$ _____

4) $13w^2v^2$ _____

5) $16pq^2$ _____

_____ %

Find the GCF for these sets of numbers.

See ASG, p. 151

1) 35, 49, 56 _____

2) 15, 21, 27 _____

3) 14, 42, 56 _____

4) 36, 60, 72 _____

5) 36, 54, 90 _____

6) 40, 64, 88 _____

7) 27, 81, 135 _____

8) 40, 60, 70 _____

9) 40, 60, 80 _____

10) 69, 115, 161 _____

_____ %

Find the GCF for these groups of monomials.

See ASG, p. 152

1) $3m, 6m, 9m$ _____

2) $5x, 10, 15x$ _____

3) $8b, 12b^2, 16b^2$ _____

4) $2y, 5y, 9y$ _____

5) $14ac, 56c^2, 28a^2c$ _____

6) $6p^2r, 12p^2, 24p^2r^2$ _____

7) $8a^3x^5, 17ax^2, 9a^2x$ _____

8) $12mnp, 18mp, 30n$ _____

9) $20xy, 30x^2y^2, 50xy^2$ _____

10) $24b^3c^2, 40b^2c^3, 72b^4c^5$ _____

11) $35x^2y^2z^2, 63x^4yz^3, 49x^3y^2z$ _____

12) $6a^3b^4, 36a^2b^3c, 54ab^2c^3$ _____

13) $18d^2f^2, 26ef^2, 34d^3e^2$ _____

14) $17x^2y^2, 11xz^3, 23yz^2$ _____

15) $18ck^2p, 45k^2p, 72ck^2$ _____

_____ %

Factor these polynomials.   See ASG, p. 153

1) $12m^2 + 4m$ _____
2) $15k^3 - 10k^2$ _____
3) $7x - 28x^2$ _____
4) $18 + 6w^3$ _____
5) $24x^2 + 18x^3$ _____

6) $16a^2c - 24ac^2$ _____
7) $18m^2np + 30np^2$ _____
8) $6rv^2u - 4mpv^2$ _____
9) $14w^2xy - 21wxy$ _____
10) $4a^2b^2c^2 + 8abc$ _____

11) $12d^2 - 8d - 4$ _____
12) $15r^3 + 5r^2 - 10r$ _____
13) $6xy^2 - 18xy - 12x$ _____
14) $14a^2b + 28ab^2 + 42ab$ _____
15) $5x^2 - 7x^3 + 12x^4$ _____
16) $6m^2np^2 - 15mn^2p^2 + 9mnp^3$ _____
17) $81r^2t^3 - 63r^2t^2 + 36r^2t$ _____
18) $81u^3v^4 + 27u^3v^3 - 54u^3$ _____
19) $6c^2e - 8c^2e^2 - 12c^3e$ _____
20) $36p^2q^3 + 44p^3q^3 + 28p^2q^2$ _____

_____ %

Tell whether or not each of these is a quadratic trinomial.   See ASG, p. 154

1) $x^3 + x^2 - 5$ _____
2) $a + 5$ _____
3) $d^2 - 2d + 4$ _____
4) $m^3 + 8m + 1$ _____
5) $3b^2 - 4b + 5$ _____
6) $5n^3 + 6n^2 - 1$ _____
7) $2y^4 - 3y + 9$ _____
8) $c - c^2 + 5$ _____
9) $-8r^2 + 3r + 2$ _____
10) $3 + t^3 - t$ _____

11) $p^2 - 3p - 18$ _____
12) $2t^7 + t^2 + 1$ _____
13) $5x + x^2 + 3x^3$ _____
14) $5 + e^2 - 2e$ _____
15) $-9u^2 + 6u + 3$ _____
16) $6s - 5s^4 + 1$ _____
17) $v + 6v^2 + 9$ _____
18) $3 - m + 4m^5$ _____
19) $2t^2 + 3t - 12$ _____
20) $w - 14 - 6w^2$ _____

_____ %

Write the pairs of factors whose product is the given number. See ASG, p. 156

1) + 4 _____
2) – 4 _____
3) + 6 _____
4) – 6 _____
5) + 8 _____
6) – 8 _____
7) + 14 _____
8) – 14 _____
9) + 24 _____
10) – 24 _____
11) + 27 _____
12) – 27 _____
13) + 30 _____
14) – 30 _____
15) + 48 _____

_____ %

Find the appropriate pair of factors. See ASG, p. 157

1) What pair of factors of + 4 add up to + 4? _____
2) What pair of factors of – 4 add up to – 3? _____
3) What pair of factors of + 6 add up to – 7? _____
4) What pair of factors of – 6 add up to + 1? _____
5) What pair of factors of + 8 add up to – 6? _____
6) What pair of factors of – 8 add up to – 7? _____
7) What pair of factors of + 14 add up to + 9? _____
8) What pair of factors of – 14 add up to – 13? _____
9) What pair of factors of + 24 add up to + 14? _____
10) What pair of factors of – 24 add up to + 5? _____
11) What pair of factors of + 27 add up to + 12? _____
12) What pair of factors of – 27 add up to – 6? _____
13) What pair of factors of + 30 add up to – 11? _____
14) What pair of factors of – 30 add up to + 7? _____
15) What pair of factors of + 48 add up to + 14? _____

_____ %

Factor these + + + trinomials.

See ASG, p. 158

1) $c^2 + 4c + 3$ _____

2) $m^2 + 5m + 6$ _____

3) $w^2 + 6w + 8$ _____

4) $x^2 + 7x + 6$ _____

5) $e^2 + 7e + 10$ _____

6) $m^2 + 7m + 12$ _____

7) $t^2 + 8t + 7$ _____

8) $u^2 + 9u + 18$ _____

9) $y^2 + 9y + 20$ _____

10) $x^2 + 10x + 9$ _____

11) $a^2 + 10a + 21$ _____

12) $b^2 + 11b + 18$ _____

13) $p^2 + 11p + 24$ _____

14) $m^2 + 11m + 28$ _____

15) $r^2 + 11r + 30$ _____

16) $p^2 + 12p + 27$ _____

17) $x^2 + 12x + 32$ _____

18) $m^2 + 13m + 22$ _____

19) $q^2 + 13q + 30$ _____

20) $c^2 + 13c + 36$ _____

21) $e^2 + 13e + 40$ _____

22) $r^2 + 13r + 42$ _____

23) $x^2 + 14x + 45$ _____

24) $b^2 + 14b + 48$ _____

25) $n^2 + 15n + 56$ _____

26) $p^2 + 16p + 48$ _____

27) $s^2 + 16s + 60$ _____

28) $x^2 + 17x + 60$ _____

29) $k^2 + 18k + 72$ _____

30) $c^2 + 20c + 75$ _____

_____ %

Factor these + − + trinomials.

See ASG, p. 159

1) $x^2 - 4x + 3$ _____

2) $b^2 - 4b + 4$ _____

3) $z^2 - 5z + 4$ _____

4) $u^2 - 5u + 6$ _____

5) $y^2 - 6y + 5$ _____

6) $w^2 - 6w + 8$ _____

7) $b^2 - 7b + 6$ _____

8) $k^2 - 7k + 10$ _____

9) $d^2 - 7d + 12$ _____

10) $w^2 - 13w + 30$ _____

11) $x^2 - 13x + 36$ _____

12) $m^2 - 32m + 60$ _____

13) $e^2 - 23e + 60$ _____

14) $g^2 - 17g + 60$ _____

15) $f^2 - 16f + 60$ _____

16) $k^2 - 35k + 96$ _____

17) $s^2 - 28s + 96$ _____

18) $n^2 - 22n + 96$ _____

19) $p^2 - 20p + 96$ _____

20) $x^2 - 29x + 100$ _____

21) $t^2 - 12t + 27$ _____

22) $u^2 - 12u + 35$ _____

23) $q^2 - 15q + 36$ _____

24) $v^2 - 15v + 50$ _____

25) $z^2 - 15z + 56$ _____

26) $r^2 - 18r + 45$ _____

27) $y^2 - 18y + 72$ _____

28) $a^2 - 18a + 80$ _____

29) $c^2 - 21c + 90$ _____

30) $d^2 - 21d + 110$ _____

_____ %

Factor these + + – trinomials.

See ASG, p. 160

1) $m^2 + 6m - 27$ _____

2) $b^2 + 6b - 40$ _____

3) $a^2 + 6a - 55$ _____

4) $z^2 + 3z - 18$ _____

5) $y^2 + 3y - 28$ _____

6) $c^2 + 3c - 40$ _____

7) $r^2 + 3r - 54$ _____

8) $f^2 + f - 12$ _____

9) $p^2 + p - 20$ _____

10) $x^2 + 12x - 28$ _____

11) $d^2 + 3d - 28$ _____

12) $w^2 + 18w - 40$ _____

13) $b^2 + 39b - 40$ _____

14) $e^2 + 19e - 42$ _____

15) $k^2 + 12k - 45$ _____

16) $v^2 + 4v - 45$ _____

17) $g^2 + 45g - 144$ _____

18) $f^2 + 32f - 144$ _____

19) $k^2 + 18k - 144$ _____

20) $u^2 + 10u - 144$ _____

21) $m^2 + 10m - 39$ _____

22) $t^2 + 10t - 96$ _____

23) $p^2 + 10p - 200$ _____

24) $m^2 + 12m - 28$ _____

25) $n^2 + 12n - 64$ _____

26) $d^2 + 12d - 108$ _____

27) $q^2 + 12q - 160$ _____

28) $c^2 + 15c - 16$ _____

29) $r^2 + 15r - 154$ _____

30) $s^2 + 15s - 250$ _____

_____ %

Factor these + – – trinomials.

See ASG, p. 161

1) $k^2 - 5k - 14$ _____

2) $h^2 - 5h - 24$ _____

3) $m^2 - 5m - 50$ _____

4) $x^2 - 8x - 84$ _____

5) $y^2 - 8y - 128$ _____

6) $z^2 - 8z - 33$ _____

7) $a^2 - 11a - 26$ _____

8) $n^2 - 11n - 60$ _____

9) $b^2 - 12b - 45$ _____

10) $z^2 - 12z - 28$ _____

11) $p^2 - 9p - 36$ _____

12) $m^2 - 5m - 36$ _____

13) $f^2 - 16f - 36$ _____

14) $q^2 - 7q - 30$ _____

15) $c^2 - 13c - 30$ _____

16) $e^2 - e - 30$ _____

17) $d^2 - 20d - 21$ _____

18) $r^2 - 4r - 21$ _____

19) $c^2 - 12c - 85$ _____

20) $d^2 - 84d - 85$ _____

21) $s^2 - 14s - 15$ _____

22) $b^2 - 14b - 51$ _____

23) $e^2 - 14e - 120$ _____

24) $t^2 - 17t - 38$ _____

25) $a^2 - 17a - 110$ _____

26) $f^2 - 24f - 112$ _____

27) $u^2 - 6u - 112$ _____

28) $g^2 - 54g - 112$ _____

29) $v^2 - 124v - 125$ _____

30) $w^2 - 20w - 125$ _____

_____ %

Identify the terms.

See ASG, p. 162

For the expression $(+x+5)(+x-3)$, which terms are the

1) Firsts? _____
2) Outers? _____
3) Inners? _____
4) Lasts? _____

For the expression $(+a-2)(+a+6)$, which terms are the

5) Firsts? _____
6) Outers? _____
7) Inners? _____
8) Lasts? _____

_____ %

F.O.I.L. these binomials.

See ASG, p. 163

1) $(k+2)(k+3)$ _____
2) $(m+1)(m+5)$ _____
3) $(v+4)(v+6)$ _____
4) $(d+8)(d-3)$ _____
5) $(u+3)(u+9)$ _____
6) $(t+5)(t-9)$ _____
7) $(e-10)(e+2)$ _____
8) $(w+6)(w+1)$ _____
9) $(f+8)(f-9)$ _____
10) $(x-11)(x-3)$ _____
11) $(g-15)(g-6)$ _____
12) $(c+19)(c-3)$ _____
13) $(s-14)(s-10)$ _____
14) $(b+13)(b-6)$ _____
15) $(n-18)(n-8)$ _____

16) $(x+5)(x-15)$ _____
17) $(c-9)(c+13)$ _____
18) $(t+16)(t+3)$ _____
19) $(r-11)(r-13)$ _____
20) $(d+5)(d-19)$ _____
21) $(h-7)(h+14)$ _____
22) $(k+12)(k+18)$ _____
23) $(v-21)(v-2)$ _____
24) $(u+13)(u-14)$ _____
25) $(z-8)(z+11)$ _____
26) $(p-16)(p-9)$ _____
27) $(a+15)(a-8)$ _____
28) $(q-11)(q+17)$ _____
29) $(r-13)(r-12)$ _____
30) $(y-20)(y-17)$ _____

_____ %

Factor these expressions.

See ASG, p. 165

1) $x^2 - 25$ _____
2) $m^2 - 49$ _____
3) $k^2 - 100$ _____
4) $w^2 - 144$ _____
5) $4c^2 - 36$ _____
6) $9w^2 - 64$ _____
7) $25y^2 - 25$ _____
8) $16c^2 - 4$ _____

9) $36n^2 - 1$ _____
10) $4p^2 - 9r^2$ _____
11) $9x^2y^2 - 16z^2$ _____
12) $a^2 - b^2$ _____
13) $n^2p^2 - 4v^2$ _____
14) $25 - x^2$ _____
15) $81 - 1$ _____

_____ %

Cancel and reduce these fractions.   See ASG, p. 169

1) $8m/8$ _____

2) $3/3p$ _____

3) $6/6xy$ _____

4) $12a/12$ _____

5) $5r/5$ _____

6) $16ce/16$ _____

7) $7/7k$ _____

8) $20/20p^2$ _____

_____ %

List the terms you can cancel in these fractions.   See ASG, p. 171

1) $\dfrac{ab}{a}$ _____

2) $\dfrac{3xy}{3y}$ _____

3) $\dfrac{c(m+n)}{d(m+n)}$ _____

4) $\dfrac{ax(p+q)}{bx(p-q)}$ _____

5) $\dfrac{xyz}{xy}$ _____

6) $\dfrac{m(n+p)}{mnp}$ _____

7) $\dfrac{ek}{e(w+r)}$ _____

8) $\dfrac{br(s+t)}{xm(s+t)}$ _____

9) $\dfrac{wcq}{c(w-q)}$ _____

10) $\dfrac{vn(c+d)}{avn(c-d)}$ _____

_____ %

Cancel and give the simplified form of these terms.   See ASG, p. 172

1) $\dfrac{ab}{a}$ _____

2) $6 - \dfrac{x}{x}$ _____

3) $\dfrac{3mn}{mn}$ _____

4) $\dfrac{p}{q} + \dfrac{q}{q}$ _____

5) $9 - \dfrac{cd}{c}$ _____

6) $\dfrac{5yz}{5z}$ _____

7) $\dfrac{a(b+c)}{3a}$ _____

8) $\dfrac{u}{v} + \dfrac{v}{v}$ _____

9) $7x - \dfrac{y}{y}$ _____

10) $\dfrac{rmq}{q}$ _____

_____ %

Good news! Not only can you factor variable terms, you can also factor numbers. For example, in a problem like $\frac{4 + 8x}{4}$, you can factor 4 out of the numerator to get $\frac{4(1 + 2x)}{4}$. Then you can cancel the 4s to get $1 + 2x$ as the final answer. And in the same way, in $\frac{5 + 15x}{10}$, you can factor 5 out of the two terms in the numerator, to get $\frac{5(1 + 3x)}{10}$. Then you can cancel the 5 in the numerator with the 10 in the denominator, to get $\frac{1 + 3x}{2}$ as the final answer.

NEW CONCEPT!

Simplify these fractions using the F.C.R. steps.

See ASG, p. 174

1) $\dfrac{6x + 12y}{6}$ _____

2) $\dfrac{ab + ac}{a}$ _____

3) $\dfrac{9m + 15n}{6}$ _____

4) $\dfrac{16}{8u - 24v}$ _____

5) $\dfrac{10s - 25t}{5}$ _____

6) $\dfrac{m}{me + mv}$ _____

7) $\dfrac{14w}{7x + 21y}$ _____

8) $\dfrac{12d - 8e + 20f}{4}$ _____

9) $\dfrac{12p - 36q}{24}$ _____

10) $\dfrac{15n + 6r - 18k}{9}$ _____

_____ %

More good news! You can factor numbers out of both the numerator and denominator. For example, in a problem like $\frac{4 + 8x}{8 - 12x}$, you can factor 4 out of both the numerator and denominator, to get $\frac{4(1 + 2x)}{4(2 - 3x)}$. Then you can cancel both 4s to get $\frac{1 + 2x}{2 - 3x}$ as the final answer.

You can even factor different numbers from numerator and denominator. For example, in $\frac{5 + 15x}{10 - 30x}$, you can factor a 5 out of the numerator, to get $5(1 + 3x)$. Then you can factor a 10 out of the denominator, to get $10(1 - 3x)$. Finally, you can cancel the 5 in the numerator with the 10 in the denominator, to get a final answer of $\frac{1 + 3x}{2(1 - 3x)}$.

NEW CONCEPT!

Reduce these fractions using the F.C.R. steps.

See ASG, p. 175

1) $\dfrac{3m + 3n}{6b + 6c}$ _____

2) $\dfrac{3 - 6y}{6 - 9y}$ _____

3) $\dfrac{7d + 21f}{14d - 21f}$ _____

4) $\dfrac{12n - 4r}{6n + 4r}$ _____

5) $\dfrac{8 + 10e}{12 + 18e}$ _____

6) $\dfrac{10 - 15m}{10m + 40}$ _____

7) $\dfrac{8a - 16c}{8a - 12c}$ _____

8) $\dfrac{2rv - 4sq}{6xy + 8wz}$ _____

9) $\dfrac{6nr + 12st}{9ns + 15rt}$ _____

10) $\dfrac{4x + 6z}{6z - 8x}$ _____

_____ %

You can simplify fractions even they have factors that are variables. For example, in the problem $\frac{3x^2 + 6x^4}{12x^3 - 4x}$, first factor the GCF in the numerator and denominator, to get $\frac{3x^2(1 + 2x^2)}{4x(3x^2 - 1)}$. Then cancel the x terms to get the final answer: $\frac{3x(1 + 2x^2)}{4(3x^2 - 1)}$.

NEW CONCEPT!

Reduce these fractions.
See ASG, p. 176

1) $\dfrac{6g^3 - 12g}{2g^3 + 2g^2}$ _____

2) $\dfrac{9y^2 - 6y}{6y^3 + 15y^2}$ _____

3) $\dfrac{4c^2 + 8c^4}{8c^3 - 2c}$ _____

4) $\dfrac{6n^3 + 9n^2}{6n^5 + 6n^3}$ _____

5) $\dfrac{12r^2 - 16r^3}{10r^2 + 30r^4}$ _____

6) $\dfrac{4a^2b + 12ab}{2ab}$ _____

7) $\dfrac{t^4 - 3t^3}{t^2}$ _____

8) $\dfrac{18u^2 - 24u^3}{6u}$ _____

9) $\dfrac{6z^3 - 9z^2}{3z^2}$ _____

10) $\dfrac{4c^3d - 6cd^2}{2cd}$ _____

_____ %

Is "x" a factor of these expressions?
See ASG, p. 177

1) $4x$ _____
2) $x + y$ _____
3) $4 + x$ _____
4) $x(5 + a)$ _____
5) $y(x + z)$ _____

6) $x - (2 + x)$ _____
7) $ax(a - x)$ _____
8) $x(x + 2)$ _____
9) $vw(x - v)$ _____
10) $vx(v - w)$ _____

_____ %

Name the factor(s) of the numerator and denominator.
See ASG, p. 178

1) $\dfrac{5(d + g)}{15(d + g)}$ _____

2) $\dfrac{n(r + t)}{r + t}$ _____

3) $\dfrac{9(e + f)}{12e}$ _____

4) $\dfrac{n + p - r}{r(n + p)}$ _____

5) $\dfrac{s - t + v}{t + v}$ _____

6) $\dfrac{x - y}{w(x - y)}$ _____

7) $\dfrac{6m^2}{(u + m)}$ _____

8) $\dfrac{4(p - q)}{6(p + q)}$ _____

9) $\dfrac{3(b + c)}{(b + c)^2}$ _____

10) $\dfrac{x^2(y - z)}{(y^2 - z^2)}$ _____

_____ %

Reduce these fractions. (Careful! You may need to factor and cancel first.)

See ASG, p. 179

1) $\dfrac{a + b}{2(a + b)}$ _____

2) $\dfrac{3(x + y)}{5(x + y)}$ _____

3) $\dfrac{m - n}{m - n}$ _____

4) $\dfrac{p + r + t}{3(p + r + t)}$ _____

5) $\dfrac{3u(v + z)}{2w(v + z)}$ _____

6) $\dfrac{9(k - 3)}{k - 3}$ _____

7) $\dfrac{s + 1}{6s + 6}$ _____

8) $\dfrac{dx + ex}{dy + ey}$ _____

9) $\dfrac{3u + 6}{7u^2 + 14u}$ _____

10) $\dfrac{4ac - 4c}{2ad^2 - 2d^2}$ _____

_____ %

Use the split-the-numerator rule, but don't simplify further.

See ASG, p. 181

1) $\dfrac{x + y}{z}$ _____

2) $\dfrac{a + b - 3}{c}$ _____

3) $\dfrac{n^2 - r}{r}$ _____

4) $\dfrac{ant - mouse}{spider}$ _____

5) $\dfrac{11 - t}{21}$ _____

6) $\dfrac{p + 2}{z}$ _____

7) $\dfrac{\bullet + \odot}{\star}$ _____

8) $\dfrac{c + d}{2}$ _____

9) $\dfrac{3v + 2u - 4x}{2x}$ _____

10) $\dfrac{k^2 - 4k}{4}$ _____

_____ %

Simplify these fractions using the split-the-numerator rule.

See ASG, p. 183

1) $\dfrac{4 + d}{d}$ _____

2) $\dfrac{c + e}{c}$ _____

3) $\dfrac{x - y}{x^2}$ _____

4) $\dfrac{p^2 - q}{q}$ _____

5) $\dfrac{a + b^2}{b^2}$ _____

6) $\dfrac{n - r^2}{r}$ _____

7) $\dfrac{v + k + w}{v}$ _____

8) $\dfrac{u + t + s}{s}$ _____

9) $\dfrac{x^2 - y^2}{x^2}$ _____

10) $\dfrac{a + b - c}{a}$ _____

_____ %

46

Identify the parts of these equations.

See ASG, p. 191

$$10y - 9 = 41 + 8y \qquad\qquad 8z - 3 = 4z + 9 - 12z$$

1) $10y - 9$ _____
2) $+41$ _____
3) $+8y$ _____
4) $41 + 8y$ _____
5) y _____

6) -3 _____
7) $8z - 3$ _____
8) $4z$ _____
9) z _____
10) $4z + 9 - 12z$ _____

_____%

Work through the simplifying phase for these equations. (You will work more with these equations on the following two pages.)

See ASG, p. 193

1) $2(a - 4) + 3a = 3a - 2$ _____
2) $4(k - 4) = 8(k + 1)$ _____
3) $4p - (p - 15) = 6(10 - p) + 4p$ _____
4) $3(b + 3) + 4b + 8 = 4(b + 8)$ _____
5) $28 - 5e = 4(10 - 3e) + 6e$ _____
6) $5(m + 4) = 2(m + 2) + 4$ _____
7) $-2(q + 8) + 2(4q - 3) = 2(4q + 3)$ _____
8) $4(3 - c) + 5c + 3 = 6c - 20$ _____
9) $6(f + 1) - 3(f + 2) = 3(2f + 3) + 6$ _____
10) $4(n - 5) + 3n - 6 = 3(n + 2)$ _____
11) $3(d - 3) - 2(1 - 3d) = 6d - 5$ _____
12) $3(r + 5) + 2(r - 2) = 2(r - 9) - 1$ _____
13) $8(s + 1) + 4s + 6 = 6(s + 3) + 2$ _____
14) $10(v - 7) + 5(4v - 6) = 26v$ _____
15) $2(5y - 2) - 22 = 11y - (3y + 6)$ _____
16) $25 - t = 46 + 3t - 3(12 + t)$ _____
17) $2(w + 17) + 5w - 1 = 2(w + 2) + 3(w + 5)$ _____
18) $4(z - 5) + 5 = -9(z + 3) + z$ _____
19) $4u - 3(u - 7) = 3(u + 11) + 3(u + 9) - 2u$ _____
20) $6(-x - 4) - 18x + 12 = 3(14 - 11x)$ _____

_____%

Solve these mini-equations.

See ASG, p. 195

1) $x + 4 = 9$ _____

2) $b + 4 = 12$ _____

3) $r + 6 = 3$ _____

4) $v + 18 = 11$ _____

5) $n - 3 = 4$ _____

6) $d - 10 = -15$ _____

7) $k - 6 = 12$ _____

8) $t - 2 = 13$ _____

9) $4 \cdot e = 24$ _____

10) $-5 \cdot q = 20$ _____

11) $8 \cdot m = -48$ _____

12) $-3 \cdot w = -21$ _____

13) $y/7 = 5$ _____

14) $f/4 = 3$ _____

15) $c/6 = -10$ _____

16) $-s/8 = 6$ _____

17) $a^2 = 36$ _____

18) $p^2 = 121$ _____

19) $u^2 = 4$ _____

20) $z^3 = 27$ _____

_____ %

Now work through the isolating phase for these equations.

See ASG, p. 197

1) $5a - 8 = 3a - 2$ _____

2) $9d - 11 = 6d - 5$ _____

3) $4k - 16 = 8k + 8$ _____

4) $3p + 15 = 60 - 2p$ _____

5) $7b + 17 = 4b + 32$ _____

6) $28 - 5e = 40 - 6e$ _____

7) $5m + 20 = 2m + 8$ _____

8) $6q - 22 = 8q + 6$ _____

9) $c + 15 = 6c - 20$ _____

10) $3f = 6f + 15$ _____

11) $7n - 26 = 3n + 6$ _____

12) $5r + 11 = 2r - 19$ _____

13) $12s + 14 = 6s + 20$ _____

14) $30v - 100 = 26v$ _____

15) $10y - 26 = 8y - 6$ _____

16) $25 - t = 10$ _____

17) $7w + 33 = 5w + 19$ _____

18) $4z - 15 = -8z - 27$ _____

19) $u + 21 = 4u + 60$ _____

20) $-24x - 12 = 42 - 33x$ _____

_____ %

Finally, work through the solving phase for these equations. See ASG, p. 198

1) $2a = 6$ _____

2) $3d = 6$ _____

3) $-24 = 4k$ _____

4) $5p = 45$ _____

5) $3b = 15$ _____

6) $-e = -12$ _____

7) $-12 = 3m$ _____

8) $28 = -2q$ _____

9) $5c = 35$ _____

10) $3f = -15$ _____

11) $4n = 32$ _____

12) $-30 = 3r$ _____

13) $6s = 6$ _____

14) $4v = 100$ _____

15) $20 = 2y$ _____

16) $-t = -15$ _____

17) $2w = -14$ _____

18) $12z = -12$ _____

19) $-39 = 3u$ _____

20) $9x = 54$ _____

_____ %

Work through the S.I.S. phases to solve these equations. See ASG, p. 199

1) $3(2a - 5) = 2(a + 10) - 15$ _____

2) $4(e + 3) + 12e = 5(e + 4) + 7(e + 5) + 5$ _____

3) $2(r + 3) = 3(4 - r) - 11$ _____

4) $2(n - 7) + 6n = 6(n + 2)$ _____

5) $2(3 - b) - 2b = 6(-b + 2) - 26$ _____

6) $5f + 4 = 5(f - 3) + 4f + 3$ _____

7) $-6(k - 7) + 3k = 2(k - 4)$ _____

8) $6(p + 10) - 3(2p + 12) = -4p + 4$ _____

9) $3(c + 3) + 6c = 3(c + 7) + 3(c + 4) - 3$ _____

10) $6(d + 6) - 8 = 2(d + 30)$ _____

11) $4(m + 5) + 4 = m + 6$ _____

12) $2(8 - q) + 5q = 5(q + 5) + 1$ _____

13) $8v + 40 = 2(3v + 10) - 2$ _____

14) $5(z + 10) + 10 = 12(z + 2) - 10z$ _____

15) $2(u - 13) = 4(16 - u)$ _____

16) $4s - 3(s + 4) = 2(2s + 3) + 9$ _____

17) $6(5 - w) = 2(w + 5) + 4$ _____

18) $2(2 - x) + 3x = 2(x + 12)$ _____

19) $4(18 - y) + 18 = 12(3 + y) - 7y$ _____

20) $5(t + 19) + 10 = 6(t + 9) - 4t$ _____

_____ %

Solve these equations.

See ASG, p. 200

1) $q/4 + 10 = 3 \cdot 5$ _____
2) $6 - r/2 = 10 - 8$ _____
3) $2(6 - 3) = (v + 5)/4$ _____
4) $5(a/3) = 2(3 + 2)$ _____
5) $p/5 = 5 - 3 \cdot 2$ _____
6) $10 - n/5 = 3 \cdot 4 - 5$ _____
7) $b/7 + 6 = 9 - 5$ _____
8) $t/3 - 7 = -10 + 2 \cdot 3$ _____

9) $-4 + u/2 = 8/4$ _____
10) $5(c/2) = -14 + 4$ _____
11) $e/2 + 7 = 4e$ _____
12) $2m - m/7 = 6 + m$ _____
13) $2x + 15 = x/2 - 3$ _____
14) $-4 + d/4 = d + 2$ _____
15) $y/5 + 3 = y/2$ _____

_____ %

Solve these equations.

See ASG, p. 201

1) $2n^2 - 9 = n^2$ _____
2) $a^2 + 4 = 13 + 7$ _____
3) $2g^2 = 4(17 + 8) + g^2$ _____
4) $p^2 - 9 = 8 \cdot 5$ _____
5) $4b^2 = 30 + 7(6 + 4)$ _____
6) $20 \cdot 5 - 19 = r^2$ _____
7) $z^2 - 5 \cdot 25 = 10^2$ _____
8) $18 + 2x^2 = 2(9 \cdot 5)$ _____

9) $5(14 + 5) = s^2 - 7^2$ _____
10) $(3c^2)/2 = 3(98)$ _____
11) $4v^2 - 64 = 3v^2$ _____
12) $-d^2 + 200 = d^2 - 42$ _____
13) $2(t^2 + 3) = t^2 + 55$ _____
14) $5 \cdot 5 = e^2/4$ _____
15) $u^2 - 9 = (24/25)u^2$ _____

_____ %

Solve — or begin solving — these absolute value equations.

See ASG, p. 202

1) $|m| = 5$ _____
2) $|n| = 8$ _____

3) $|3r - 4| = 13$ _____
4) $|10 - y| = 1$ _____

_____ %

Solve these absolute value equations.

See ASG, p. 203

1) $|2a - 3| = 9$ _____
2) $|1 - 3k| = 10$ _____
3) $|2n + 5| = 3$ _____
4) $|6(b + 1)| = 18$ _____
5) $|4r + 6| = 10$ _____

6) $|12 - 3e| = 6$ _____
7) $|8c - 3| = 5$ _____
8) $|10 - 5t| = 15$ _____
9) $|2d + 2| = d + 10$ _____
10) $|4p - 6| = p + 9$ _____

_____ %

Solve these quadratic trinomials equations. **See ASG, pp. 204–205**

1) $v^2 + 6v + 8 = 0$ _____

2) $m^2 - 4m - 12 = 0$ _____

3) $u^2 - 10u + 21 = 0$ _____

4) $t^2 + 4t - 32 = 0$ _____

5) $s^2 + 8s + 15 = 0$ _____

6) $x^2 - 4x - 45 = 0$ _____

7) $k^2 - 9k + 20 = 0$ _____

8) $c^2 + 5c - 84 = 0$ _____

9) $r^2 + 7r + 6 = 0$ _____

10) $y^2 - 9y - 22 = 0$ _____

11) $w^2 - 15w + 54 = 0$ _____

12) $p^2 + 6p - 7 = 0$ _____

13) $z^2 + 12z + 32 = 0$ _____

14) $q^2 + 8q - 20 = 0$ _____

15) $n^2 - 10n - 75 = 0$ _____

_____ %

Find the length of the hypotenuse of each right triangle (round to the tenths place, if necessary). **See ASG, p. 209**

1) legs have lengths 2 cm. and 6 cm. _____

2) legs have lengths 4 inches and 10 inches _____

3) legs have lengths 5 miles and 12 miles _____

4) legs have lengths 7 feet and 24 feet _____

5) legs have lengths 9 meters and 15 meters _____

6) legs have lengths 7 inches and 18 inches _____

7) legs have lengths 5 feet and 21 feet _____

8) legs have lengths 9 yards and 40 yards _____

9) legs have lengths 11 lightyears and 60 lightyears _____

10) legs have lengths 10 mm. and 23 mm. _____

_____ %

Find the length of the second leg of each right triangle (round to the tenths place, if necessary). **See ASG, p. 210**

1) leg = 2 yards, hypotenuse = 3 yards _____

2) leg = 4 meters, hypotenuse = 5 meters _____

3) leg = 5 feet, hypotenuse = 13 feet _____

4) leg = 6 cm., hypotenuse = 9 cm. _____

5) hypotenuse = 17 mm., leg = 10 mm. _____

6) hypotenuse = 25 inches, leg = 7 inches _____

7) hypotenuse = 10 feet, leg = 6 feet _____

8) leg = 9 miles, hypotenuse = 41 miles _____

9) hypotenuse = 16 yards, leg = 12 yards _____

10) leg = 7 meters, hypotenuse = 9 meters _____

_____ %

Graph these points on two sets of coordinate axes. See ASG, p. 218

COORDINATE PLANE A

A) $(-3, 4)$
B) $(4, -5)$
C) $(5, 2)$
D) $(2, 4)$
E) $(-2, -3)$
F) $(0, 1)$
G) $(-1, 2)$
H) $(-5, -2)$
J) $(1, -3)$
K) $(-4, 1)$

COORDINATE PLANE B

A) $(2, -4)$
B) $(-8, -2)$
C) $(4, 6)$
D) $(6, -8)$
E) $(-3, 5)$
F) $(0, -6)$
G) $(-10, -7)$
H) $(5, 2)$
J) $(10, -7)$
K) $(-1, 9)$

State the values for x_1, y_1, x_2, and y_2. See ASG, p. 221

1) P_1 is $(6, -8)$, P_2 is $(7, -4)$ _____
2) P_1 is $(1, 4)$, P_2 is $(-5, -6)$ _____
3) P_1 is $(3, -7)$, P_2 is $(3, 11)$ _____
4) P_1 is $(5, 2)$, P_2 is $(9, 2)$ _____
5) P_1 is $(6, 9)$, P_2 is $(12, -4)$ _____
6) P_1 is $(7, -1)$, P_2 is $(-6, 14)$ _____
7) P_1 is $(4, 6)$, P_2 is $(1, -3)$ _____
8) P_1 is $(-2, 1)$, P_2 is $(2, 6)$ _____
9) P_1 is $(-3, -8)$, P_2 is $(4, -9)$ _____
10) P_1 is $(0, 4)$, P_2 is $(-6, -10)$ _____

_____ %

_____ %

Find the slope of the line passing through these points.   See ASG, p. 222

1) (4, 2) and (8, 4)   _____

2) (9, 1) and (6, 4)   _____

3) (3, -1) and (7, 0)   _____

4) (-4, -2) and (-2, 2)   _____

5) (5, 3) and (-1, 9)   _____

6) (-4, 2) and (-2, 10)   _____

7) (7, 8) and (8, 11)   _____

8) (0, -2) and (10, -6)   _____

9) (-3, 3) and (-4, 13)   _____

10) (0, 1) and (1, 2)   _____

_____ %

Given one point (P_1) and the slope (m), graph the lines on two coordinate planes.   See ASG, pp. 224–225

COORDINATE PLANE A

a) $P_1 = (-4, 4)$, m = 1

b) $P_1 = (6, 4)$, m = 1/2

c) $P_1 = (-4, -6)$, m = 3/4

d) $P_1 = (5, -2)$, m = 1/5

e) $P_1 = (0, 3)$, m = 2/3

COORDINATE PLANE B

f) $P_1 = (0, 0)$, m = 2

g) $P_1 = (-3, 4)$, m = 1/4

h) $P_1 = (2, -5)$, m = 2/5

j) $P_1 = (-9, -5)$, m = 3/4

k) $P_1 = (-6, 0)$, m = 7

_____ %

Given one point (P_1) and the slope (m), graph the lines on two coordinate planes.   See ASG, pp. 226–227

COORDINATE PLANE C

l) $P_1 = (1, 3)$, m = -1/3

m) $P_1 = (-5, 1)$, m = -3

n) $P_1 = (8, -8)$, m = -2/5

p) $P_1 = (3, -2)$, m = -3/4

q) $P_1 = (-7, -6)$, m = -1/6

COORDINATE PLANE D

r) $P_1 = (-3, 4)$, m = -5/3

s) $P_1 = (7, 6)$, m = -1/6

t) $P_1 = (-5, -6)$, m = -10

u) $P_1 = (9, -6)$, m = -2/3

v) $P_1 = (-2, -4)$, m = -1/7

_____ %

Name the x- and y-intercepts for each of these lines.   See ASG, p. 229

_____ %

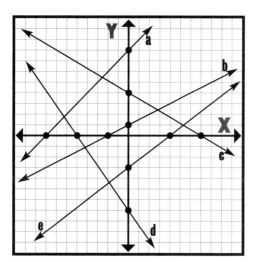

COORDINATE PLANE A

a) _____

b) _____

c) _____

d) _____

e) _____

_____ %

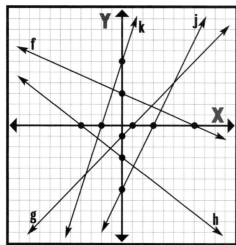

COORDINATE PLANE B

f) _____

g) _____

h) _____

j) _____

k) _____

Name the slopes and y-intercepts of these lines.   See ASG, p. 230

1) $y = 3x + 8$ _____

2) $y = -4x + 2$ _____

3) $y = \frac{1}{2}x - 4$ _____

4) $y = 2x + \frac{1}{2}$ _____

5) $y = -\frac{3}{5}x + 3$ _____

6) $y = 6x + 1$ _____

7) $y = -8x - \frac{4}{5}$ _____

8) $y = x - 2$ _____

9) $y = -\frac{9}{10}x + \frac{3}{2}$ _____

10) $y = \frac{1}{4}x$ _____

11) $y = 7x + 2$ _____

12) $y = -2x - \frac{1}{5}$ _____

13) $y = \frac{1}{8}x - 6$ _____

14) $y = -\frac{5}{8}x + \frac{2}{3}$ _____

15) $y = -x - 3$ _____

16) $y = 5$ _____

17) $y = -2x + \frac{1}{2}$ _____

18) $y = \frac{1}{4}x + 10$ _____

19) $y = \frac{1}{6}x - 4$ _____

20) $y = -8x - 1$ _____

_____ %

Graph these lines on four coordinate planes. See ASG, pp. 231–232

a) $y = 3x$

b) $y = \frac{1}{3}x + 2$

c) $y = -\frac{3}{2}x - 5$

d) $y = \frac{1}{2}x - 2$

e) $y = -\frac{2}{3}x + 1$

f) $y = \frac{4}{5}x + 3$

g) $y = \frac{3}{4}x + 4$

h) $y = 6x + 4$

j) $y = -\frac{1}{4}x + 4$

k) $y = \frac{1}{2}x + 5$

l) $y = \frac{1}{2}x + 1$

m) $y = \frac{1}{2}x - 4$

_____ %

Given one point (P$_1$) and the slope (m), write the equation of the line. See ASG, p. 233

1) $P_1 = (2, 4)$, m = 2 _____

2) $P_1 = (2, -7)$, m = 3/5 _____

3) $P_1 = (5, 8)$, m = 1/2 _____

4) $P_1 = (-3, 8)$, m = -1 _____

5) $P_1 = (9, 12)$, m = 1/3 _____

6) $P_1 = (-8, -2)$, m = 2 _____

7) $P_1 = (-4, 6)$, m = -3 _____

8) $P_1 = (-1, 7)$, m = 2/9 _____

9) $P_1 = (5, -10)$, m = -2 _____

10) $P_1 = (0, -3)$, m = 5/8 _____

_____ %

Given two points, write the equation of the line. See ASG, p. 234

1) $(4, -7)$ and $(8, -1)$ _____

2) $(6, -3)$ and $(-3, 15)$ _____

3) $(6, 3)$ and $(8, 0)$ _____

4) $(3, -4)$ and $(9, 2)$ _____

5) $(15, 3)$ and $(5, -1)$ _____

6) $(-2, 10)$ and $(5, -25)$ _____

7) $(1, 12)$ and $(-2, -12)$ _____

8) $(-1, 4)$ and $(-5, 7)$ _____

9) $(4, 10)$ and $(-2, -8)$ _____

10) $(-3, 7)$ and $(-5, 2)$ _____

_____ %

Write these equations in slope-intercept form.

See ASG, p. 235

1) $-6x + 3y = 18$ _____

2) $16 + 2y = 6x$ _____

3) $14 - 7y = 21x$ _____

4) $5x - 5y = 10$ _____

5) $3y + 6x = 4$ _____

6) $9 - 4y - 2x = 1$ _____

7) $7y + 5x = 5$ _____

8) $6x - y = 10$ _____

9) $12 + 3y = 8x$ _____

10) $6y - 36 = 9x$ _____

11) $15x - 21 = 5y$ _____

12) $3(x + y) = 9$ _____

13) $8x = 5(y + 2)$ _____

14) $9y - 3x + 3 = 0$ _____

15) $14x + 3y = -15$ _____

16) $2 + 3y = 11 - x$ _____

17) $3x + y = 5x - 4$ _____

18) $7y - 5 = 3x + 2y$ _____

19) $8(x - 2) = 3(x + 2y)$ _____

20) $4(x - y) = 7(x + 2) - y$ _____

_____ %

Write the equations of these lines, then graph them on two coordinate planes.

See ASG, p. 236

COORDINATE PLANE A

a) the vertical line through $(4, 0)$ _____

b) the horizontal line through $(-3, 2)$ _____

c) the vertical line through $(-6, 3)$ _____

d) the horizontal line through $(-3, -3)$ _____

COORDINATE PLANE B

e) the horizontal line through $(-6, 3)$ _____

f) the vertical line through $(2, 4)$ _____

g) the horizontal line through $(5, -2)$ _____

h) the vertical line through $(-3, -5)$ _____

_____ %

Solve these pairs of equations (find the intersection point). See ASG, pp. 238–239

1) $2y + 2x = 6$
$y + 6x = -7$ _____

2) $5y + 8 = 2x$
$2x + y = 20$ _____

3) $5x - 3 = 4y$
$2y + 3x = -7$ _____

4) $3y = x - 18$
$y + 4x = 7$ _____

5) $y + 2x = -4$
$y + 9 = 3x$ _____

6) $y = 2x + 6$
$y + 10 = 4x$ _____

7) $3x + 2y = 9$
$2x + 3y = 6$ _____

8) $x - 8y = 4$
$4y + 4x = 52$ _____

9) $6x + 2 = y$
$4y - 3x = -34$ _____

10) $2x + 3y = 6$
$2y - x = 4$ _____

11) $3y + x = -4$
$y + 2x = 2$ _____

12) $3x + 2y = 18$
$7x + 3y = 32$ _____

13) $y - 2x = 9$
$3y + 6 = -5x$ _____

14) $y = 2x + 25$
$3y + x = 5$ _____

15) $3y - 7x = 15$
$x - 3y = 3$ _____

16) $2y = x + 16$
$5y + 2x = 40$ _____

17) $2y + 7x = -32$
$3x - 12 = 2y$ _____

18) $y + 18 = 3x$
$5y + 3x = 0$ _____

19) $9x - 2y = 7$
$y + 2x = 16$ _____

20) $y + 3 = 4x$
$4y + x = 22$ _____

_____ %

Solve each pair of equations to find the intersection point. Then graph the lines to confirm that they intersect there. See ASG, p. 240

1) $x + y = 1$
$2y - x = 8$ _____

2) $y - x = -1$
$y - 2x = -2$ _____

3) $y - 3x = 3$
$y + 2x = -2$ _____

4) $3y - x = 6$
$x - y = 0$ _____

5) $5x - 2y = 12$
$3x + 2y = 4$ _____

6) $x - y = 2$
$2x + y = -8$ _____

7) $5y - 3x = 10$
$5y - 2x = 15$ _____

8) $2y - x = 12$
$4x + y = -3$ _____

9) $y - 3x = 2$
$3y + x = 6$ _____

10) $6x + y = -3$
$y - 2x = 5$ _____

_____ %

Find the distance between each pair of points.   See ASG, p. 242

1) (5, 5) and (2, 1) _____
2) (3, 8) and (8, -4) _____
3) (2, -8) and (-5, -16) _____
4) (10, 8) and (6, 2) _____
5) (2, 6) and (-1, 1) _____

6) (5, 3) and (7, -3) _____
7) (5, -2) and (-1, -10) _____
8) (-3, -7) and (-1, 0) _____
9) (-5, -4) and (3, 7) _____
10) (5, 7) and (-4, -5) _____

_____ %

— Interesting Historical Fact —

The distance formula is based on the world-famous, and still-very-much-used Pythagorean Theorem. This formula was originally used way back in the days of Ancient Egypt to help landowners figure out where the property lines started and stopped.

Write these phrases using algebraic symbols.

See ASG, pp. 248–249

1) Four less than a number. _____

2) Eight more than a number. _____

3) Eighteen more than a number. _____

4) Eighteen less than a number. _____

5) Sixty less than a number. _____

6) Three times a number. _____

7) Seven less than the opposite of a number. _____

8) Six times the opposite of a number. _____

9) Three times the quantity of five less than three times a number. _____

10) Ten more than four times the opposite of a number. _____

11) The opposite of the quantity of three less than two times a number. _____

12) Nine less than six times a number. _____

13) Nine less than six times the opposite of a number. _____

14) Six times the quantity of nine less than a number. _____

15) Nine times the quantity of six less than three times a number. _____

_____ %

Translate these statements into equations, but don't solve them.

See ASG, p. 250

1) Eight more than a number equals three times the number. _____

2) What percent of twenty is nine? _____

3) The sum of two consecutive integers is fifteen. _____

4) What percent of forty is ten? _____

5) Three times the quantity of two more than a number is twenty-one. _____

6) Two times the quantity of six less than a number equals the opposite of the number. _____

7) Nine is thirty percent of what number? _____

8) A number equals three times the quantity of five less than twice the number. _____

9) The opposite of the quantity of one more than two times a number equals five. _____

10) The sum of three consecutive integers is thirty-three. _____

11) Six times a number divided by five equals two more than the number. _____

12) What percent of eighty is sixteen? _____

13) The sum of four consecutive integers is eighteen. _____

14) The opposite of four times a number equals ten more than the number. _____

15) Thirty divided by a number equals one less than the number. _____

_____ %

Solve for the variable in these word problems.

See ASG, p. 251

1) Two more than three times a number equals eleven. _____

2) Five times the quantity of one less than two times a number equals twenty-five. _____

3) Thirteen times a number equals four times the quantity of five more than two times the number. _____

4) Four times the quantity of six more than twice a number equals twice the number. _____

5) Three more than two times a number equals six more than the opposite of the number. _____

6) Six more than four times a number equals eight less than three times the number. _____

7) Four times the quantity of eight less than the opposite of a number is three more than three times the number. _____

8) Seven times the quantity of twenty less than four times a number is eight times the number. _____

9) Five times the quantity of six less than a number is two times the quantity of three more than the number. _____

10) Four less than ten times a number is fourteen times the number. _____

_____ %

Solve these percent word problems.

See ASG, p. 252

1) What percent of 60 is 12? _____
2) What percent of 50 is 5? _____
3) 4 is what percent of 200? _____
4) What percent of 56 is 14? _____
5) 45 is what percent of 36? _____

6) What percent of 40 is 36? _____
7) 76 is what percent of 100? _____
8) 54 is what percent of 27? _____
9) What percent of 5 is 2? _____
10) 24 is what percent of 30? _____

_____ %

Solve these percent increase problems.

See ASG, p. 253

1) What's the result when 75 is increased by 20%? _____

2) What's the result when 60 is increased by 30%? _____

3) 40 gets increased by 5%. What's the result? _____

4) What's the result when 12 is increased by 50%? _____

5) 2 gets increased by 50%. What's the result? _____

6) What's the result when 15 is increased by 200%? _____

7) What's the result when 56 is increased by 25%? _____

8) 300 gets increased by 45%. What's the result? _____

9) What's the result when 120 is increased by 70%? _____

10) 80 gets increased by 35%. What's the result? _____

_____ %

Solve these consecutive integer problems.
See ASG, p. 254

1) Two consecutive integers add up to 9. What are they? _____
2) Two consecutive even integers add up to 26. What are they? _____
3) Three consecutive integers add up to 24. What are they? _____
4) Three consecutive even integers add up to 30. What are they? _____
5) Four consecutive integers add up to 54. What are they? _____
6) Two consecutive odd integers add up to 76. What are they? _____
7) Four consecutive even integers add up to 52. What are they? _____
8) Three consecutive odd integers add up to 129. What are they? _____
9) Five consecutive integers add up to 85. What are they? _____
10) Four consecutive odd integers add up to 64. What are they? _____

_____ %

Solve these age problems.
See ASG, p. 256

1) Eli is three years older than Jon. Two years ago, Eli's age was four times Jon's age. How old is Eli now? _____
2) Chris is five times as old as Zac. In thirty years, Chris will be twice Zac's age. How old is Zac now? _____
3) Dawn is four years younger than Melanie. Five years ago, Melanie was twice Dawn's age. How old is Melanie now? _____
4) Paul is six years older than Corinne. Ten years ago, twice Paul's age was triple Corinne's age. How old is Paul now? _____
5) Debbie is 16 years younger than Asher. Three years from now, Asher will be three times as old as Debbie. How old is Asher now? _____

_____ %

Solve for the third quantity.
See ASG, p. 258

1) r = 15 mph; t = 3 hours _____
2) t = 2 hours; d = 18 miles _____
3) d = 50 miles; r = 25 mph _____
4) t = 6 hours; d = 72 miles _____
5) r = 60 mph; t = 5 hours _____
6) d = 100 miles; t = 5 hours _____
7) t = 8 hours; r = 3 mph _____
8) r = 15 mph; d = 75 miles _____
9) d = 117 miles; t = 9 hours _____
10) r = 36 mph; d = 90 miles _____

_____ %

Solve these $d_1 = d_2$ problems.

See ASG, pp. 260–261

1) Stacy rode her bike away from home for 3 hours at 8 miles per hour, but then she got a flat tire. Her dad drove out to pick her up, but it only took him 1 hour to get there. How fast did Stacy's dad drive? _____

2) Antoine drives from Chicago to Minneapolis to visit his aunt. He drives for 6 hours at 60 miles per hour. On the way home, bad weather forces him to drive 45 miles per hour. How long will the return trip take? _____

3) Esteban is a long-distance runner who runs for 5 hours at 9 kilometers per hour. Tony is a skateboarder who skates at 15 kilometers per hour. How long does it take Tony to cover the same distance? _____

4) Rachel skis down a mountain at 1500 feet per minute for 20 minutes. The ski lift takes 50 minutes to return her to the top. How fast does the ski lift travel? _____

5) Every day, Sisyphus is forced to roll a boulder up a mountain at 1 mile per hour for 16 hours. Every night, he slips at the top and the boulder rolls back down the mountain in 15 minutes (1/4 of an hour). How fast does the boulder roll down the hill? _____

_____%

Solve these $d_1 + d_2 = d_{total}$ problems.

See ASG, pp. 262–263

1) Sarah leaves her house on her bike, headed west at 8 miles per hour. Her brother, Mark, leaves on foot, headed east at 3 miles per hour. How far apart will they be after 4 hours? _____

2) Rebecca and Luke live 200 miles apart. If they leave their houses at the same time, Luke driving at 40 miles per hour and Sarah driving at 60 miles per hour, how long will it be until they meet? _____

3) Naomi leaves Dallas on a train heading north at 75 miles per hour. At the same time, John leaves Dallas on a train heading south. After three hours, they are 420 miles apart. How fast is John's train going? _____

4) Alex and Isabel leave St. Louis at the same time, heading in opposite directions. If Alex travels at 12 miles per hour and Isabel travels at 16 miles per hour, how many hours pass before they are 168 miles apart? _____

5) Jacob lives 18 miles away from Beth. They leave their houses at the same time, aiming to meet somewhere in between. If they end up meeting 6 miles from Beth's house after 2 hours, how fast does Jacob walk? _____

_____%

Given the answer to the subtraction problem, determine if your set-up should be   Larger Number – Smaller Number or   Smaller Number – Larger Number.

See ASG, p. 270

1) Answer is 8
2) Answer is - 8
3) Answer is - 6
4) Answer is 3/5
5) Answer is 6/8
6) Answer is - 0.003
7) Answer is - 0.385
8) Answer is 5.23

_____ %

Find the pair of numbers with the given sum and difference.

See ASG, pp. 271-272

1) Sum = 20, difference = 4
2) Sum = 18, difference = 8
3) Sum = 16, difference = 8
4) Sum = 25, difference = 3
5) Sum = 28, difference = 4
6) Sum = 28, difference = 18
7) Sum = 18, difference = 14
8) Sum = 27, difference = 3
9) Sum = 24, difference = 4
10) Sum = 30, difference = 20

_____ %

Find the pair of numbers with the given sum and difference.

See ASG, pp. 273-274

1) Sum = 33, difference = - 7
2) Sum = - 20, difference = - 2
3) Sum = - 18, difference = - 4
4) Sum = 0, difference = - 26
5) Sum = 5, difference = - 3
6) Sum = 13, difference = - 25
7) Sum = 2, difference = - 28
8) Sum = 23, difference = - 123
9) Sum = 100, difference = - 300
10) Sum = 30, difference = - 40

_____ %

For each situation, let a variable stand for the smaller unknown. Then create an expression that stands for the larger unknown.

See ASG, p. 275

 _____%

1) Paul has 50 times as many apples as Sam.
2) Kyle travels 30 miles farther than Zane travels.
3) Abigail has 80 more coins than Ethan.
4) Ned scores 3 more goals than Ted.
5) Daniel eats 3 times faster than Jacob.
6) Avril gains 30 points more than Mason.
7) Noah solves a problem 5 times faster than Liam solves it.
8) Shyan consumes 1,000 more calories than Jack.
9) Karyn gains her energy 8 times faster than Alexander gains his energy.
10) Jayden speaks twice as fast as Sophia.

For each situation, let a variable stand for the smaller unknown. Then create an expression that stands for the larger unknown.

See ASG, p. 276

 _____%

1) Ben is five times shorter than Ned.
2) Paul's savings account has a balance that's 2 times smaller than Ted's savings account balance.
3) Samuel's speed is 3 times less than Jack's speed.
4) Javier loses 3 times less weight than Alexander loses.
5) Madison drinks 5 times less fruit juice than William drinks.
6) Sam drives 13 mph slower than Avril drives.
7) Zombies eat 7 times fewer "things" than aliens eat.
8) In a game of "Candy Crash," Sophia scores 5,000 fewer points than Isabella.
9) Juan's has 300 fewer Facebook friends than Emily.
10) As a daily average, Ava drinks 2 fewer cups of coffee than Mia.

Write an algebraic expression to express the value of each set of coins, in cents:

See ASG, p. 277

 _____%

1) An unknown number of nickels.
2) An unknown number of nickels added to an unstated number of dimes.
3) An unstated number of nickels added to an unknown number of quarters.
4) The difference of an unknown number of half-dollars minus an unspecified number of dimes.
5) The difference of an unknown number of quarters minus an unstated number of dimes.
6) An unknown number of half-dollars added to an unspecified number of nickels.
7) The difference of an unstated number of nickels minus an unspecified number of half-dollars.
8) The difference of an unstated number of dimes minus an unspecified number of quarters.
9) The difference of an unknown number of nickels minus an unspecified number of dimes.
10) The difference of an unstated number of dimes minus an unspecified number of nickels.

For each situation, first write the ME/E. Then, using the Master Formula for the value of coins, convert the ME/E into the ME/M.

See ASG, p. 279

_____ %

1) Emma has dimes and nickels with a total value of $9.85.

2) Gabriella has $6.70 in dimes and half-dollars.

3) Felix's saving bank holds half dollars and nickels with a total value of $96.65.

4) Ted's nickels and dimes have a total value of $8.80.

5) When Giovani counts up the value of his quarters and dimes, he finds that their value is $9.95.

6) Albert has $2.75 in quarters and half-dollars.

7) Daniela's piggy bank contains $7.20 in dimes and quarters.

8) Sandra's safe holds $93.35 in nickels and half-dollars.

9) Antonio has nickels and quarters totalling $32.95.

10) Javier has $102.00 in dimes and quarters.

Solve each coin problem. Remember that after writing the ME/E and ME/M, you must substitute so that the equation you get contains just one variable.

See ASG, pp. 280-281

_____ %

1) Paul has 10 fewer quarters than nickels. His coins have a total value of $36.20. How many quarters and how many nickels does Paul have?

2) Betty has 9 more dimes than quarters, and her coins have a total value of $4.40. How many quarters and how many dimes does Betty have?

3) Ben's money chest contains half-dollars and dimes, with 7 more dimes than half-dollars. If the total value of Ben's coins is $14.50, how many of each kind of coin does Ben have?

4) Jenni has 7 fewer dimes than nickels, and her coins have a total value of $2.30. How many nickels and dimes does Jenni have?

5) Ken has $7.50 in dimes and nickels. He has 9 more dimes than nickels. How many dimes and how many nickels does Ken have?

_____ %

Solve, using approach for MULTIPLICATION-related unknowns: See ASG, pp. 282-283

1) Damien's piggy bank contains nickels, quarters and dimes. The number of nickels is 7 times the number of dimes, and the number of quarters is 3 times the number of dimes. If Damien's coins have a $3.60 value, how many nickels, quarters and dimes does Damien have?

2) Arianna gives money to her friend. She gives 19 times as many quarters as nickels. Arianna gives a total of $33.60 in coins. How many quarters and how many nickels does Arianna give her friend?

3) Brian's loose change jar holds 3 times as many dimes as half dollars and twice as many nickels as dimes. If the jar holds $5.50, how many of each kind of coin does the jar contain?

4) When Jason empties his pocket, he sees that he has $3.15 with twice many dimes as quarters. How many quarters and dimes does Jason have?

5) Julio smashes open her piggy bank, and out comes a flood of half-dollars, dimes and nickels. The number of half-dollars is 4 times the number of nickels, and the number of dimes is twice the number of half-dollars. Jake's coins have a value of $28.50. How many nickels, dimes and half-dollars does Julio have?

Express the TOTAL-related unknowns in both possible ways.   See ASG, p. 284

_____ %

1) Kim has a total of 37 nickels and dimes.

2) Davis has 89 coins in quarters and dimes.

3) Zara has 23 coins in quarters and nickels.

4) Ben has a total of 71 coins in quarters and half-dollars.

5) Malachi has 10 coins in dimes and pennies.

6) Allen has 32 coins in pennies and nickels.

7) Jasmine has 98 coins in half-dollars and pennies.

8) Kiara has 13 coins in half-dollars and dimes.

Solve, using the approach for TOTAL-related unknowns: See ASG, pp. 285-286

_____ %

1) Diego has $14.75 in nickels and quarters with a total of 75 coins. How many does he have of each kind of coin?

2) Greg has $15.30 in half-dollars and dimes with a total of 53 coins. How many of each kind of coin does Gret have?

3) Carlos has $6.25 in silver-dollars and nickels with a total 30 coins. How many does he have of each kind of coin?

4) Eli has $8.75 in nickels and half-dollars with a total of 40 coins. How many of each kind of coin does Eli have?

5) Alice has $8.00 in nickels and quarters with a total of 60 coins. How many does she have of each kind of coin?

Solve each problem, using the approach on pp. 289-290.   **See ASG, pp. 289-290**

_____%

1) Mr. Williams informs his science class that their weekly test consists of both 4-point long-answer questions and 2-point short-answer questions. The test, worth 60 points, contains 25 questions. How many questions are of the long-answer type, and how many are of the short-answer type?

2) Gym teacher Travis Rounds buys equipment for his high school's baseball team. He buys bats for $100 each and packs of a dozen baseballs for $50 each. If Travis buys 20 items in all for a total of $1,750, how many bats and packs of a dozen balls does he buy?

3) The Eagles team beats its opponent 85-0. The Eagles score 20 times through both net goals (5 points each) and bonus goals (2 points each). How many bonus goals and net goals do the Eagles score?

4) Tickets to a musical production cost $25 for children and $50 for adults. Spending $1,625, Daniel buys 40 tickets to the production for company employees and their children. How many of each kind of ticket does Daniel purchase?

5) At a farmer's coop, Ethan buys sacks of rice for $5 apiece and sacks of flour for $10 apiece. He buys 12 sacks for a total cost of $95. How many sacks of rice and flour does Ethan buy?

For each phrase, determine if the variables are related by ADDITION, MULTIPLICATION, or by a TOTAL.   **See ASG, p. 291**

_____%

1) Mia has 8 times as many storybooks as Tia.

2) Jordan and Jake have a total of 20 pairs of shoes.

3) Henry's car runs 5 mph faster than Ben's car runs.

4) The "Buy-Now-Bargain" Auto Lot offers 300 cars in all, some new, the rest used.

5) Jack's father is 30 years older than Jack.

6) Brock is twice as tall as his toddler child, James.

7) The Adams Middle School's library contains 1,500 books, some fiction, and the rest non-fiction.

8) Vera's mom is 24 years older than Vera.

9) Eva's ranch contains sheep and goats with 200 animals in all.

10) Emma can correctly spell words 4 times faster than her friend Jennifer can spell them.

11) Sophia is 3 years younger than her sister Margerie.

12) Madison's wardrobe allows her to create 20 outfits, some for spring or summer, the rest for fall or winter.

For each problem, do the three steps shown on p. 292.   **See ASG, p. 292**

1) Ned's accuracy in solving math problems is 3 times greater than Jed's accuracy.

2) The top speed of Ken's car is 20 mph greater than the top speed of Jennifer's car.

3) Bob has a collection of 13 car and truck toys.

4) Daryn can throw a baseball 6 times faster than Karyn can throw it.

5) Sal weighs 20 pound less than Ben weighs.

6) Evan scores 25 fewer points in a round of bowling than Todd scores.

7) Arlen can long jump 2 times farther than Joey can long jump.

8) Bo has 9 books, with some on math topics, the rest on science topics.

9) Matt scores 3 fewer goals than Pat scores.

10) Gwen devours jelly beans 4 times faster than Max does.

11) Swen's score on a video game is 120,000 points higher than Hal's score.

12) Newt's home has a total of 29 doors and windows.

_____%

For each situation, which Master Equation would you use: $d_1 = d_2$ or $d_1 + d_2 = d_T$?   **See ASG, p. 293**

1) Jacob and Mason start back-to-back, then run in opposite directions.

2) Daniel walks from northeast to southwest, then he returns to his starting point.

3) William walks from the ground floor of a building to the 5th floor. Then he descends, returning to the ground floor.

4) Cameron hits a baseball twice. Each hit travels the same distance.

5) Two dogs are 300 yards apart. They run toward each other and stop when they meet.

6) Jayden bikes from home to school. Heading back, he walks from school to home.

7) As she travels from school to home, Sophia first skips 1/3 of the way. Then she jogs the remaining 2/3 of the trip.

8) Two friends are 200 miles apart. They drive toward each other and their cars eventually meet.

9) A postman drives her route on Wednesday. She drives the same route on Thursday.

10) Two friends start out together and walk in opposite directions. After three hours they are 8 miles apart.

_____%

Given each situation, answer the THREE QUESTIONS: See ASG, p. 294
   a) Which Master Equation would you use?
   b) Which unknown should the variable stand for?
   c) How are the unknowns related to each other?

1) Noah drives from his home to a park at 7 mph, then he drives back home at 5 mph. How long does it take Noah to go to the park if his round-trip takes half an hour?

2) Emma bikes from her home to the food coop, then bikes from the coop to a friend's house. Emma's speed biking to her friend's house is 3 mph slower than her speed biking to the coop. If Emma's entire trip takes 2.5 hours, how fast does she bike during each leg of her trip?

3) Mia takes 1.5 hours to bike from home to the library, then another 2 hours to bike to a hiking trail. If her rate going to the hiking trail is 2 times faster than her rate from home to the library, and if the entire trip is 20 miles, how fast does Mia bike during each leg of her trip?

4) Jackson bikes from home to the mall at 4 mph. Bicycling from the mall back home, he travels at 10 mph. How much time does Jackson spend biking each way if his time going is 2 hours more than his time returning?

5) To gather supplies, Shayna rides her horse from her mountain ranch to the nearby town, then returns to the ranch. Riding to town, Shayna's speed is 4 mph, but on the trip back she travels 2 mph. How long does it take Shayna to travel each way if her round trip takes 5 hours?

Solve each problem, using the approach on pp. 295-296.   See ASG, pp. 295-296

1) Max jogs from his home to the bank in 10 minutes and runs back home in 5 minutes. If his rate running home is 5 hectometers per minute (hpm) faster than his rate jogging to the bank, what are Max's two rates?

2) Canadian triathletes Jed and Peg, training for their next triathlon, run a 48-kilometer race. Jed takes 6 hours to complete the race while Peg takes 8 hours to complete it. If Jed's rate is 2 kilometers per hour (kph) faster than Peg's rate, what are the rates of Jed and Peg?

3) Ivan and Luke, longtime friends and ardent bikers, attend seaside colleges 90 kilometers apart. They plan to leave their respective colleges at the same time, bike and meet at Sunshine City, a beach town between the schools. If Ivan biking speed is 6 kph faster than Luke's, and if the friends reach Sunshine City in 3 hours, what are the biking speeds of Ivan and Luke?

4) Rayna and Leah leave together from Leah's house and motorcycle separately, but along the same route, to a picnic area. Rayna reaches the picnic area in 36 minutes (= 0.6 hours), while Leah reaches it in 24 minutes (= 0.4 hours). If Leah's speed is 30 kilometers per hour faster than Rayna's, what are their two speeds, in kph?

Answer the Three Questions, then use approach on 297-298.   **See ASG, pp. 297-298**

1) Two friends, long separated, run towards each other for an embrace. The first friend runs 12 feet per second (fps) while the second runs 9 fps. Their two running times, combined, sum to 8 seconds. If the two friends run across 87 feet in all, for how many seconds does the first friend run? For how many seconds does the second friend run?

2) Ken and Ben, football players on opposing teams, spot a fumbled ball at the same instant. Dashing to recover the ball, Ken sprints for 5 seconds, while Ben runs for 4 seconds. Ben's speed in yards per second (yps) is twice Ken's speed, and the two boys run a total of 26 yards when they reach the ball at the same moment. How fast do Ken and Ben run in yards per second?

3) Janet and Graham are 550 miles apart when they decide to drive to Gainesville, a town between them, where they'll attend the Gen Con gamers' convention. Janet drives 75 miles per hour (mph), and Graham drives 65 mph. If Graham drives 2 hours more than Janet, how long does each person drive by the time they arrive at Gen Con?

4) Sandy's car develops problems when she's 240 miles away from home, so she calls home to inform her mom. Sandy limpingly drives toward home, and her mom leaves in her own car to meet Sandy on the highway. They meet after the mom has driven two hours and Sandy has driven four hours. If Sandy's mom drives four times as fast as Sandy, how fast was Sandy driving, and how fast was her mom driving?

Answer the Three Questions, then use approach on 299-300.   **See ASG, pp. 299-300**

1) Starting at the same station, two trains head apart in opposite directions, train 'A' heading north and train 'B' steaming south. Train 'B' travels 20 mph faster than Train 'A.' After 1.5 hours, the trains are 180 miles apart. What is the speed of each train in miles per hour?

2) After meeting for a reunion in Albuquerque, Sara and Emma drive in opposite directions, Emma heading east, and Sara heading west at a speed 15 mph faster than Emma's speed. If Sara and Emma are 435 miles apart after 3 hours of driving, what are their individual speeds?

3) Daniel has a pair of toy cars, a Purple Ferrari and a Yellow Lambo, that he can make move in opposite directions. Daniel makes the Purple Ferrari go 2 feet per second (fps) faster than the Yellow Lambo. After just 3 seconds, the cars are 24 feet apart. What are the speeds of Daniel's two cars in feet per second?

4) Ned and Ted start biking in opposite direction from the same starting point, with Ned's speed 4 feet per second (fps) slower than Ted's speed. If Ned and Ted cover a total distance of 400 feet in 25 seconds, what is the speed of each boy?

Find the plane's speed with the tailwind and against the headwind. **See ASG, p. 302**

1) Plane's speed in still air = 740 mph;
   wind's speed = 36 mph.

2) Plane's speed in still air = 885 kph;
   wind's speed = 47 kph.

3) Plane's speed in still air = 608 mph;
   wind's speed = 29 mph.

4) Plane's speed in still air = 789 kph;
   wind's speed = 54 kph.

 _____ %

Using elimination technique, solve each pair of equations. **See ASG, pp. 303-304**

1) Equation A: $2p + 8q = -12$
   Equation B: $4p + 7q = -15$

2) Equation A: $6a + 2b = -6$
   Equation B: $-3a - 8b = -39$

3) Equation A: $2v + 3w = 4$
   Equation B: $3v + 4w = 7$

4) Equation A: $3c - 4e = -9$
   Equation B: $c + 6e = -25$

 _____ %

Simply set up both Master Equations for each problem, including the given distance. DON'T solve. **See ASG, p. 305**

1) A boat, sailing with the current, takes 1 hour to travel the 300 miles from San Francisco to Santa Barbara, California. The same boat, sailing against the current, takes 1.5 hours to make the return trip.

2) Flying with a tailwind, a plane takes 3 hours to fly the 1,700 miles from Austin, Texas, to Boston, Massachusetts. On the return trip the same plane, now fighting a headwind, takes 4 hours.

_____ %

Solve, using the technique on pp. 306 - 307.

See ASG, pp. 306-307

_____ %

1) Flying into a headwind, a passenger plane travels 2,200 miles in 5 hours. Aided by a tailwind, the same plane makes the return trip in 4 hours. What is the speed of the plane in still air, and what is the speed of the wind?

2) Traveling against the current, a boat makes the 450-mile trip from Charleston to Miami in 18 hours. Traveling with the current, the same boat makes the return trip in 15 hours. What's the speed of the boat in still water, and what's the speed of the current?

Express the amount of work completed in each situation.

See ASG, p. 308

_____ %

1) Kathy can build a treehouse in 6 weeks, and she works on one for 2 weeks.

2) Josie can animate a cartoon in 2 weeks, and she works on one for 1 week.

3) Ari can cook dinner in 3 hours, and he works on it for 2 hours.

4) Steve can clean his room in 60 minutes, and he works on it for 15 minutes.

5) Ella can write a song in 5 hours, and she works on one for 4 hours.

Write the ME/E and the ME/M for each situation.

See ASG, p. 309

1) Ashlynn takes 7 hours to paint a 10' x 10' room, while Nadia needs 9 hours to complete the same task. How long will it take the two of them to paint this same size room if they work together?

2) Candace can prepare breakfast for six people in 45 minutes, but it takes Sarah 1 hour to prepare the same meal. How long will it take them to make this same breakfast if they work together?

3) Two birds are building a nest. Working alone, the first bird takes 4 days to build a nest. The second bird needs only 2 days to build her nest. How long will it take the birds to build a nest if they work together?

4) A man completes The New York Times crossword puzzle in 9 minutes, but his daughter can complete the same puzzle in just 3 minutes. Assuming seamless cooperation, how long would it take father and daughter to solve the puzzle if they work on it together?

5) Noah requires 3 days to paint the fence that surrounds his house, while Adam needs only 2 days to do the same task. How long would it take the two of them to complete this task if they work together?

Solve for the variable.

See ASG, p. 310

1) $1/8\, x + 5/6\, x = 1$

2) $1/3\, x + 3/4\, x = 1$

3) $2/5\, x + 1/2\, x = 1$

4) $1/6\, x + 1/5\, x = 1$

5) $4/5\, x + 9/10\, x = 1$

6) $2/9\, x + 1/6\, x = 1$

_____ %

Solve these work problems.

See ASG, pp. 3111-312

1) Valerie can make a piñata in 3 hours. Danielle, new to the business, requires 5 hours to make a piñata. Danielle works on her piñata for 2 hours when Valerie starts to help her with it. How long will it take the two of them, working together, to finish the piñata?

2) Justin can eat a whole pizza in 18 minutes, but it takes Victor only 12 minutes to eat the same size pizza. Justin starts eating a pizza for 10 minutes, then asks Victor to help him finish it. How long does it take the two boys, eating together, to finish this pizza?

3) Rowan's mother can peel a bag of carrots in 25 minutes. But Rowan, who dislikes working in the kitchen, takes 50 minutes to peel the carrots. Rowan peels the carrots for 15 minutes before her mother decides to help. How long will it take the two of them, working together, to finish peeling the carrots?

_____ %

Given the situation, write the ME/E and ME/M. Don't Solve!

See ASG, p. 313

1) It takes 2 hours for an air conditioner to cool down a house. If the air conditioner is not on, an open window will warm the house up in 5 hours. How many hours will it take to cool the house down if the air conditioner is running but one window is left open?

2) It takes Deborah 1 hour to rake the leaves. On a windy day, the falling leaves will cover the lawn in 6 hours. How long does it take Deborah to rake the leaves on a windy day?

3) It takes a stove 15 minutes to heat up a pot of soup. A forgetful chef leaves the lid off, which can cool the soup in 50 minutes. How many minutes will it take to heat up the pot of soup if the lid is left off?

4) Zack needs 45 minutes to sweep the floor. His pet dog, shedding tremendously, can cover the floor is 3 hours. How many minutes will it take Zack to sweep the floor if his dog is shedding on the floor?

_____ %

Solve the following work problems.

See ASG, pp. 314-315

1) An air conditioner cools down an auditorium in 30 minutes. The stage lights can heat up the stage in 90 minutes. If the stage lights are left on and the air conditioner is running, how many minutes will it take for the stage to cool down?

2) The bathtub faucet will fill the tub in 7 minutes. But the drain, when fully open, will empty the tub in 35 minutes. How long will it take to fill the tub if the drain is fully open?

3) Justin starts a fire in the fireplace. It normally takes 14 minutes for the fire to warm up the house. But today he forgot to close the panoramic window which, when left open, cools the house down in 21 minutes. How many minutes will it take for the house to warm up with the fire going and the window open?

Calculate the amount of pure substance in each solution.

See ASG, p. 316

1) You have 80 ml of a 75% solution of acetic acid.

2) A bottle contains 140 ml of a 10% solution of benzoyl peroxide.

3) A chemistry class buys 3 quarts of a 32% citric acid solution.

4) A beaker contains 55 ml of a 90% solution of hydrochloric acid.

5) You have 1 liter of a 65% solution of lactic acid.

6) A bottle contains 48 ml of a 45% solution of magnesium hydroxide.

Write the ME/E and the ME/M for each of the following problems. But don't solve the problems.

See ASG, p. 317

1) Caitlyn needs to dilute a 65% solution of lactic acid to a 38% solution. She has 14 quarts of the 65% lactic acid solution and can add any amount of a 20% lactic acid solution. How many quarts of the 20% lactic acid solution should Caitlyn add to correctly dilute her solution?

2) Nick restores painted wooden furniture and needs a 52% solution of sodium hydroxide to remove paint so he can varnish the wood. He has 40 ml of a 10% sodium hydroxide solution and wants to boost this solution to a 52% concentration by adding some of an 85% sodium hydroxide solution. How many milliliters of the 85% solution should Nick add to reach his target concentration?

3) Betsy needs to make a solution that's 60% acetone to remove stains caused by permanent markers. She has 300 ml of an 80% acetone solution and needs to add a certain volume of 45% acetone. How many milliliters of the 45% solution should Betsy add to attain her desired 60% solution?

4) To develop photographs, Raphael needs a solution that's 15% citric acid. He has 4.1 liters of a 75% citric acid solution, and he can add any amount of 5% citric acid solution. How many liters of the 5% citric acid solution should Raphael add to reach his desired 15% concentration?

5) Stacy wants to create a rubbing alcohol solution with a concentration of 43%. She has 84 ml of a 20% solution and a limitless supply of a 66% solution. How many milliliters of the 66% solution should Stacy add to the 20% solution to reach her goal?

Solve the following mixture problems.   **See ASG, pp. 318-319**

1) Suzana is working on her car and needs to make a 28% ether solution. She has 3 liters of a 35% solution. How many liters of a 12% ether solution does Suzana need to add to make her solution the right strength?

2) Caleb is going camping and wants to make an iodine solution to sterilize his water. He has 2 cups of 88% iodine concentrate and a limitless amount of a 5% iodine solution. Caleb needs a 26% iodine solution in order for it to be effective. How many cups of the 5% solution does Caleb need to add?

3) Iris' car engine runs most efficiently when it uses 96-octane gasoline. Iris has 9 gallons of 98-octane gasoline. How many gallons of 92-octane gas should Iris add to make her car run with greatest efficiency? *[Note: the octane number is the percent of octane in the gasoline.]*

 ____%

Solve the mixture problems.   **See ASG, pp. 320-321**

1) Camille wants to make her oatmeal sweeter. To be precise, she wants the oatmeal to have a sugar concentration of exactly 10%. She has 1 cup (= 16 tablespoons) of oatmeal with a 5% sugar concentration. How many tablespoons of pure sugar should Camille add to make the oatmeal the way she likes it?

2) Raquel has made 8 cups of her favorite stir fry when she runs out of peas. At this point, her stir fry is only 14% peas. But for it to be perfect, Raquel knows that the stir fry should contain 26% peas. How many cups of pure peas should Raquel add to the stir fry (after she buys or borrows them) so that it reaches the correct 26% concentration of peas?

3) Aimee needs an alloy that's 60% gold to make a batch of golden earrings for holiday presents. She has 5 oz of an alloy that is only 11% gold. How many ounces of pure gold should Aimee add to boost the alloy's concentration to the ideal 60% level?

____%

Solve the mixture problems.   **See ASG, pp. 322-323**

1) Carl craves lots of M&M's in his trail mix. He wants a mixture that's 15% M&M's but his mixing bowl is filled with 3 cups (24 ounces) of a mix that's only 8% M&M's. How many ounces of this 8% mixture should Carl remove and replace with pure M&M's to boost his trail mix to the desired 15% M&M level?

2) For a painting project, Astrid is trying to create a shade of baby blue that's 45% white. But after accidentally squeezing out too much blue paint, Astrid determines that the 20 ml of paint she has created is too blue, being only 22% white. How many milliliters of this 22%-white paint should Astrid remove and replace with 100% white paint to make her color the desired 45% white shade?

3) Ian Budds, proprietor of Tempting Teas, is creating a new blend of chai tea that needs to be 78% Darjeeling tea. After making 8 cups of his first batch, Ian finds it's too weak, as it's only 63% Darjeeling. How many cups of this blend does Ian need to remove and replace with pure Darjeeling tea to boost the blend up to the 78% strength?

 ____%

Hey! What's this thing?

And how do I use it?

In this box you write the percent of the problems you got right in each section.

And just how do you figure that out? Well, if you know how percents work, you'll be able to figure this out. If you don't yet know this skill, just use the handy chart below. You need two pieces of information:

1)   the number of problems in the section, and

2)   the number of problems you answered correctly (find this by scoring your work against the answer key in the back of the Workbook).

To find your percent correct, just multiply the number you got right by the "magic %" number in the chart.

HANDY DANDY CHART

If the section has this many problems:	the "magic %" number is:
4	25
5	20
8	12.5
10	10
20	5
25	4
50	2

Example: Suppose a section you did has 20 problems, and you got 15 right. Looking at the chart, you see that you need to multiply 15 by 5. This means you got 75% correct. Put that number in the percent box, and that tells how you did. That is it!

But what if a section has a strange number of problems, like 8, 12, 15, 30, or 70? Aha! Just divide the number you got right by the total number of problems, then multiply the answer by 100. And the answer is the percent you got right.

Quick example: a section has 70 problems, and you got 59 right. 59 divided by 70 equals about 0.84. Multiplying 0.84 by 100, you get 84%. Voilà, you got 84% of those problems right.

1) Reflexive
2) None
3) Symmetric
4) Transitive
5) None
6) Symmetric
7) Transitive
8) None
9) None
10) Symmetric

1) Distributive
2) Associative
3) Commutative
4) Distributive
5) Commutative
6) None
7) Distributive
8) None
9) Associative
10) Associative

1) Multiplicative identity
2) Additive identity
3) Multiplicative identity
4) None
5) Additive identity
6) None
7) None
8) None
9) Multiplicative identity
10) Additive identity

1) N, W, I
2) I
3) N, W, I
4) W, I
5) I
6) None
7) I
8) N, W, I
9) None
10) None

11) N, W, I
12) N, W, I
13) None
14) I
15) None
16) N, W, I
17) I
18) N, W, I
19) I
20) None

1) R
2) I
3) I
4) R
5) I
6) R
7) R
8) I
9) R
10) R

11) R
12) I
13) R
14) R
15) I
16) I
17) R
18) I
19) R
20) I

1) +3
2) +7
3) −10
4) +8
5) −12
6) −3
7) +13
8) +15
9) −10
10) −11

11) +19
12) −21
13) −21
14) +25
15) +17
16) −25
17) +42
18) −39
19) −30
20) +34

21) +14
22) +14
23) −16
24) +24
25) −26
26) −20
27) +18
28) +27
29) +45
30) −56

31) +10
32) −20
33) −30
34) +40
35) +28
36) −30
37) −23
38) +26
39) +58
40) −33

41) +25
42) +18
43) +10
44) −25
45) −40
46) +21
47) +40
48) −46
49) +66
50) −79

1) +1
2) +1
3) −3
4) +2
5) +6
6) −2
7) +2
8) +1
9) +4
10) +2

11) −5
12) +1
13) +2
14) −3
15) −3
16) −6
17) +5
18) +6
19) +8
20) +1

21) −3
22) −32
23) −16
24) −10
25) +40
26) +13
27) +6
28) −9
29) +9
30) −18

31) −10
32) +7
33) +13
34) −30
35) +14
36) +10
37) +40
38) −36
39) −28
40) +45

41) +8
42) +31
43) −1
44) +15
45) +15
46) +21
47) −45
48) +4
49) −24
50) +25

51) −100
52) +2
53) +32
54) −80
55) +203
56) +362
57) +500
58) −269
59) +366
60) +489

61) −37
62) −689
63) −275
64) −313
65) +362
66) +692
67) +176
68) +400
69) +109
70) −302

1) S, −10	11) M, +7	1) +3	11) +36
2) M, −4	12) S, +21	2) +4	12) +16
3) S, +10	13) M, +13	3) −5	13) −80
4) M, +4	14) S, −20	4) 0	14) +30
5) M, −3	15) S, +21	5) +2	15) +30
6) M, +3	16) S, +45	6) +15	16) −41
7) S, −13	17) M, −10	7) −44	17) −35
8) S, +13	18) M, +8	8) +16	18) +131
9) M, −4	19) M, −3	9) −20	19) +448
10) S, +13	20) M, +4	10) −16	20) −288

page 10

1) +10	1) −5	1) +37	11) +20	21) +5
2) −21	2) +6	2) +3	12) −56	22) +73
3) +27	3) +17	3) +4	13) −45	23) −79
4) −60	4) −9	4) −31	14) +24	24) −23
5) −45	5) +28	5) +11	15) −49	25) +151
		6) +14	16) +73	26) −94
		7) +52	17) +76	27) +27
		8) −9	18) −91	28) +34
		9) +56	19) +24	29) +122
		10) −54	20) −7	30) −25

page 11

1) −3 − 2, S, −5	10) −4 − 6, S, −10	19) −76 + 63, M, −13
2) −8 + 5, M, −3	11) +12 + 8, S, +20	20) +21 + 81, S, +102
3) +7 + 4, S, +11	12) −7 − 17, S, −24	21) −126 − 804, S, −930
4) −9 − 7, S, −16	13) +24 − 9, M, +15	22) +312 − 392, M, −80
5) +6 − 7, M, −1	14) +4 + 31, S, +35	23) +181 + 406, S, +587
6) +8 + 4, S, +12	15) −46 − 8, S, −54	24) −240 − 376, S, −616
7) −7 + 3, M, −4	16) +27 − 35, M, −8	25) +621 + 412, S, +1,033
8) +2 − 2, M, 0	17) −61 + 45, M, −16	
9) −1 + 8, M, +7	18) −86 − 52, S, −138	

page 12

1) −11	11) −3	1) −6
2) −7	12) −37	2) −24
3) −1	13) −81	3) +56
4) 0	14) −99	4) −52
5) −4	15) +75	5) +64
6) −4	16) −129	6) +48
7) +11	17) +177	7) −448
8) +7	18) −126	8) +486
9) −2	19) −83	9) −300
10) −4	20) −194	10) +68

1) − 8
2) + 3
3) − 4
4) + 20/6 or +10/3
5) + 5
6) + 23
7) − 19/4
8) + 7
9) − 8
10) − 9

1) Parentheses before exponents, + 81
2) Parentheses before multiplication, + 18
3) Exponents before mixed-sign rule, − 12
4) Parentheses before exponents, + 4
5) Exponents before multiplication, + 144
6) Grouping before mixed-sign rule, − 8
7) Division before same-sign rule, + 10
8) Parentheses before mixed-sign rule, − 2
9) Parentheses and exponents before mixed-sign rule, − 20
10) Exponents before same-sign rule, + 40

1) First ( ), then [ ]
2) First ( ), then { }
3) First { }, then [ ], then ( )
4) First ( ), then { }, then [ ]
5) First ( ), then ||
6) First [ ], then ( ), then { }
7) First [ ], then ( ), then ||
8) First ||, then ( ), then { }
9) First ||, then { }, then [ ]
10) First ( ), then [ ] , then { }

1) 64
2) − 38
3) 46
4) 3
5) − 5
6) 13
7) − 34
8) 49
9) 25
10) − 5

11) − 20
12) 9
13) 0
14) 43
15) 4
16) − 2
17) − 7
18) 4
19) − 6
20) 15

1) 20
2) 20
3) 5
4) 5
5) 125
6) 125
7) 125
8) 9
9) 9
10) 4

11) 1
12) 42
13) 42
14) 42
15) 1
16) 16
17) 1
18) 1
19) 9
20) 1/4

1) 18
2) 16
3) 32
4) 36
5) 48
6) 144
7) 225
8) 28
9) 98
10) 100

1a) 36
2a) 64
3a) 64
4a) 144
5a) 144
6a) 72
7a) 45
8a) 196
9a) 196
10a) 20

1) − 4
2) − 9
3) − 16
4) − 25
5) − 36
6) 49
7) 64
8) − 81
9) 100
10) − 121

1a) 4
2a) 9
3a) 16
4a) 25
5a) 36
6a) − 49
7a) − 64
8a) 81
9a) − 100
10a) 121

1) Yes
2) No
3) No
4) Yes
5) No
6) Yes
7) No
8) Yes
9) Yes
10) No

1) 5m
2) q
3) rmx
4) 3ab
5) $2c^2d$
6) mr
7) $2z^2$
8) $2t^2v$
9) 0
10) $5x^2z$

1) 6a
2) 5x
3) 4m
4) 5r
5) 3c
6) 6y
7) 0
8) f
9) $5r^2$
10) 2mn

For example, 4 apples + 2 apples = 6 apples
For example, 3 eggs + 2 eggs = 5 eggs
For example, 6 monkeys − 2 monkeys = 4 monkeys
For example, 4 rhinos + 1 rhino = 5 rhinos
For example, 5 cats − 2 cats = 3 cats
For example, 4 yolks + 1 yolk + 1 yolk = 6 yolks
For example, 2 babies − 2 babies = 0 babies
For example, 6 frogs − 3 frogs − 2 frogs = 1 frog
For example, 2 rats + 3 rats = 5 rats
For example, 4 men − 2 men = 2 men

1) +10x
2) −19y
3) +26m
4) −22a
5) −28q

1) −5n
2) −9p
3) −5c
4) +13d
5) −7r

1) +19f
2) −15x
3) −4c
4) −28h
5) −5e
6) +5d
7) +21w
8) −8x
9) +17v
10) −27b

11) −9d
12) −37a
13) +15z
14) +7m
15) −32r
16) +41u
17) +23t
18) −31q
19) −15c
20) +2m

21) −11b
22) +45s
23) −37p
24) +9k
25) +46h
26) −40n
27) −9a
28) +16j
29) +42g
30) −7y

page 18

1) 3mn
2) −3mq
3) −8rx
4) −bcx
5) 2rx^2
6) −3dq^2
7) 2mp
8) 0
9) 2fv
10) −3gh

11) 6pt
12) r^{2}nw
13) −4qx
14) 3b^{2}c
15) −2def
16) 2r^{2}nz
17) 0
18) 3.1p^2
19) −28pqr^2
20) 2bdf^2

1) 3x + 2y
2) 2
3) −q + 4
4) 6bc + df
5) −xz + 2
6) −hn − bq
7) −3m + 5.2
8) 2y^2 − 2y
9) 8cd^2 − 2f
10) 4xy + $\frac{1}{3}$

11) 3np − 2pr
12) 0
13) 6qh − 3qt
14) 6p
15) 4ty − 4
16) 4r^2 − 2pr
17) 5n^{2}x + 4.3
18) 4xy + 3yz
19) −7r^2 − 2mt
20) 5r^{2}qb + 2rqb

page 19

1) a + b
2) a − b
3) −a − b
4) −a + b
5) −y − 6
6) y − 6
7) y + 6
8) −y + 6
9) −3 − g
10) −6 + m

11) −3 + x
12) −n − p − 2
13) p + r − 3
14) −a + b + c
15) 2 − q
16) m − n + p
17) −d − e + 6
18) x + y + z
19) p − q − r
20) a + 4 − c

1) a + 5
2) 1 − b
3) c + 3
4) d + 3
5) e − 3
6) −f
7) −g − 4
8) −h − 2
9) j − 1
10) k − 18

11) −m
12) n + 15
13) p + 15
14) 3 − q
15) r − 10
16) −s − 3
17) t
18) −u − 15
19) 4 − v
20) −w

page 20

1) 4
2) 4
3) 2/3
4) 42
5) 1.6
6) 7.25
7) 7.25
8) 5/6
9) 5/6
10) 9

1) 2
2) 20
3) 20
4) 12
5) 6
6) 6
7) 2
8) 0
9) 12
10) 24

1) 7
2) −1
3) 4
4) 3
5) −3
6) 6
7) 6
8) −6
9) 10
10) 2

11) −3
12) −10
13) 12
14) 0
15) −4

1) −6
2) 3
3) 16
4) −2
5) −5
6) −50
7) 3
8) 24
9) −1
10) 9

11) 10
12) −13
13) 144
14) 4
15) −14
16) 36
17) −16
18) 5
19) 3
20) −25

1) 5
2) −8
3) −9
4) 7
5) 9
6) 7
7) −2
8) 1
9) 2
10) −2

1) 9
2) $n \cdot n$
3) $n \cdot n \cdot n$
4) 8
5) $(4x) \cdot (4x) = 16x^2$
6) 27
7) $b \cdot b \cdot b$
8) 64
9) $(pq) \cdot (pq) = p^2 q^2$
10) $\left(\frac{1}{4}\right) \cdot \left(\frac{1}{4}\right) = \frac{1}{16}$

1) 3^{10}
2) w^8
3) 4^{m+n}
4) 6^6
5) aardvark^7
6) p^9
7) 4^{11}
8) $2^{hip+hop}$
9) r^{12}
10) 6^{x+y}

11) 10^{20}
12) a^{15}
13) $\triangle^{15}$
14) c^{15}
15) 12^{10}
16) t^{5n}
17) a^{b+c}
18) $\diamondsuit^9$
19) 87^{36}
20) $(xy)^{w+z}$

1) 3^4
2) w^4
3) 5^4
4) $\bullet^5$
5) 8^{a-b}
6) a^8
7) tic$^{tac-toe}$
8) $(p+q)^{r-s}$
9) $\heartsuit^7$
10) $m^{d-d} = m^0 = 1$

1) $8y^2$
2) $42p^3$
3) $6m^4$
4) $25b^7$
5) $32x^5$
6) $12v^2$
7) $12t^9$
8) $12a^{10}$
9) $54f$
10) $50c^6$

11) $40w$
12) $15e^4$
13) $4y^2$
14) $24p^4$
15) $30x^6$

1) $2m$
2) $3r^2$
3) $4p^3$
4) $5q^4$
5) $3m^8$
6) 2
7) e^2
8) y
9) $\frac{3}{2}t^4$
10) 1

11) $6p^{x-y}$
12) $7d^8$
13) $2c^5$
14) $2x^6$
15) $4d^3$

1) 3
2) 1
3) 1
4) −10
5) 1
6) π
7) 1
8) 12
9) 162
10) 1

1) a^4
2) 5
3) 11
4) $x^2 y^4$
5) $a + 2$
6) mn^2
7) $4mn^2$
8) $r^2 - 1$
9) $\frac{a^3 b^2 c}{xz^4}$
10) 5/9

1) $y - 3$
2) $y^2 + 2y - 6$
3) $-m^2 - m + 3$
4) $2b^3 + 3b^2 - 3b - 4$
5) $n^2 + 13$
6) $2c^2 - c + 3$
7) $-2p^4 - 3p^3 + p^2 + 6p + 9$
8) $x^5 - 3x + 7$
9) $a^3 - 2a^2 + 9a - 5$
10) $3e^2 - 2e + 5$

11) $8r^4 - 3r^3 + r^2 - r + 4$
12) $12t^3 + 2t^2 - t + 5$
13) $-3q^2 - 5q + 5$
14) $8w^5 + 3w^4 - 4w^3 - 2w^2 - w + 6$
15) $-s^3 - s^2 + s + 5$

page 25

1) $1/x^2$
2) $1/b^4$
3) $1/c^8$
4) $1/\diamond^5$
5) $1/81$
6) $1/7^n$
7) $1/12^{earring}$
8) $1/y^x$
9) $1/cat^{dog}$
10) $1/8^m$

1) 2^7
2) p^6
3) 3^x
4) $\oplus^w$
5) $ski^{snowboard}$
6) r^6
7) 8^c
8) $pizza^{slice}$
9) $\diamond^3$
10) 7

1) $\dfrac{3}{x^2 y^3}$
2) $\dfrac{x^3}{y^2}$
3) $\dfrac{2m^2 r^3}{5n^4 p^4}$
4) $7a^2 b^3 c^5$
5) $\dfrac{e^3}{d^2}$
6) $\dfrac{r^2 j^8}{f^3 x^5}$
7) $\dfrac{6p^2}{r^2}$
8) $\dfrac{36n^2 x^3 r^2}{p^4 m^2}$
9) $\dfrac{25xy^2 n^2}{9m^3}$
10) $\dfrac{d^x e^y f^z}{a^n b^m c^p}$

page 26

1) 2^4
2) x^7
3) $\dfrac{1}{4^3}$
4) $\dfrac{1}{clone^5}$
5) m^8
6) z^{13}
7) $\dfrac{1}{10^8}$
8) $lemur^3$
9) $\dfrac{1}{r}$
10) $\dfrac{1}{n^7}$

1) $\dfrac{1}{r^9}$
2) m^5
3) $\dfrac{1}{3^{24}}$
4) x
5) eel^{13}
6) c^{20}
7) $\dfrac{1}{z^5}$
8) $\dfrac{1}{pony^{11}}$
9) 6^5
10) $\dfrac{1}{v}$

1) $\dfrac{a^6}{b}$
2) $\dfrac{r^6}{3^1} = \dfrac{r^6}{3}$
3) $4^1 w^8 = 4w^8$
4) $\dfrac{v^6}{t^2}$
5) $\dfrac{1}{8^2 n^7} = \dfrac{1}{64n^7}$
6) 1
7) $5^3 d^7 = 125 d^7$
8) $\dfrac{1}{9^2 z^{11}} = \dfrac{1}{81 z^{11}}$
9) $\dfrac{u^6}{k^5}$
10) $7^1 = 7$

page 27

1) 3^8
2) a^{15}
3) c^{xy}
4) 4^6
5) $llama^{16}$
6) k^{-8}
7) $\odot^{30}$
8) p^{-xz}
9) gum^{36}
10) n^{24}
11) 6^{10}
12) 12^{-18}
13) $\diamond^{cf}$
14) 3^{27}
15) p^{4r}
16) 8^{-48}
17) v^{20}
18) $\star^{-vw}$
19) e^{-28}
20) bug^{-3d}

1) e^9
2) $2^3 p^9 = 8p^9$
3) x^5
4) $(-2)^2 r^6 = 4r^6$
5) $\dfrac{1}{b^5}$
6) $\dfrac{4^2}{z^{18}} = \dfrac{16}{z^{18}}$
7) $\dfrac{t^9}{5^1} = \dfrac{t^9}{5}$
8) $\dfrac{1}{k^{38}}$
9) v^{10}
10) $\dfrac{3^2}{r^{15}} = \dfrac{9}{r^{15}}$
11) w
12) c^{21}
13) $\dfrac{n^9}{4^3} = \dfrac{n^9}{64}$
14) $3^2 y^5 = 9y^5$
15) 1
16) $\dfrac{1}{5^3} = \dfrac{1}{125}$
17) $\dfrac{f^{17}}{6^2} = \dfrac{f^{17}}{36}$
18) $\dfrac{1}{s^7}$
19) $\dfrac{8^1}{q^2} = \dfrac{8}{q^2}$
20) $\dfrac{u^6}{4^2} = \dfrac{u^6}{16}$

page 28

1) $3^2 \cdot 5^2$
2) $x^4 \cdot y^4$
3) $4^{-p} \cdot 7^{-p}$
4) $a^x \cdot b^x$
5) $tooth^4 \cdot eye^4$
6) $6^{-d} \cdot 3^{-d}$
7) $2^3 \cdot 4^3 \cdot 5^3$
8) $\triangle^z \cdot \square^z$
9) $p^{-2} \cdot q^{-2}$
10) $c^y \cdot e^y$

1) $25y^2$
2) $8z^3$
3) $9a^2$
4) $64b^3$
5) $9n^2$
6) $-8d^3$
7) $36c^2$
8) $16h^2$
9) $125e^3$
10) $49f^2$
11) $64g^2$
12) $-8b^3$
13) $216p^3$
14) $8r^3$
15) $16t^2$
16) $81a^4$
17) $49k^2$
18) $-216m^3$
19) $16z^4$
20) $64j^3$
21) $27w^3$
22) $36x^2$
23) $343y^3$
24) $256p^4$
25) $-729n^3$
26) $27q^3$
27) $-64u^3$
28) $-512s^3$
29) $8v^3$
30) $1000x^3$

page 29

1) $\dfrac{1}{b}$

2) $\dfrac{ec^4}{7^2} = \dfrac{ec^4}{49}$

3) $\dfrac{1}{w^7}$

4) $\dfrac{q^5}{p}$

5) $\dfrac{n^6}{3^1} = \dfrac{n^6}{3}$

6) $\dfrac{3^2 z^8}{t^2} = \dfrac{9z^8}{t^2}$

7) $\dfrac{y^4}{9^2 x^{11}} = \dfrac{y^4}{81x^{11}}$

8) $\dfrac{y^{12}}{k}$

9) $a^9 c^{11}$

10) $6^2 d^2 m^5 = 36 d^2 m^5$

1) $\dfrac{m^6}{n^6}$

2) $\dfrac{2^3}{5^3}$

3) $\dfrac{\triangle^x}{\square^x}$

4) $\dfrac{t^c}{w^c}$

5) $\dfrac{3^{-2}}{7^{-2}}$

6) $\dfrac{2^3}{9^3}$

7) $\dfrac{x^{-3}}{y^{-3}}$

8) $\dfrac{r^{-p}}{c^{-p}}$

9) $\dfrac{\bigstar^{\triangle}}{\square^{\triangle}}$

10) $\dfrac{3^{-4}}{10^{-4}}$

1) $\dfrac{r}{m^2}$

2) $\dfrac{1}{bc^5}$

3) $\dfrac{t^7}{3^2 w^7} = \dfrac{t^7}{9w^7}$

4) $\dfrac{a^2}{c^2}$

5) $2^1 e^4 = 2e^4$

6) $\dfrac{v^3}{n^3}$

7) $\dfrac{5^3 r}{d^2} = \dfrac{125r}{d^2}$

8) $\dfrac{b^5}{c^8}$

9) $\dfrac{m^8 n^2}{7}$

10) $\dfrac{1}{2^3 \cdot 5^2} = \dfrac{1}{200}$

page 30

1) 4
2) 5
3) 2
4) 8
5) 7
6) 10
7) 9
8) 13
9) 11
10) 14

1) 25
2) 12a
3) $7mn^2$
4) w
5) 1/4
6) c
7) 19
8) 36xy
9) salami
10) $16p^2 q^2$

1) 18
2) m
3) rt
4) 1/8
5) ☺
6) q
7) $8w^2$
8) mnp
9) $100x^2 y$
10) magic

1) 169
2) y^2
3) 961
4) 225
5) r^4
6) 1/25
7) $144p^2$
8) 324
9) 12,321
10) $100x^2 y^2$

page 31

1) $-2\sqrt{8}$
2) $-6\sqrt{7}$
3) $10\sqrt{4} = 10 \cdot 2$
4) $13\sqrt{2}$
5) $-13\sqrt{12}$
6) $-9\sqrt{u}$
7) $9\sqrt{v}$
8) $-21\sqrt{a}$
9) $-16\sqrt{t}$
10) $17\sqrt{x}$

1) $\sqrt{10}$
2) $\sqrt{21}$
3) $\sqrt{ac}$
4) $\sqrt{dx}$
5) $\sqrt{6y}$
6) $\sqrt{13a}$
7) $\sqrt{\text{frog} \cdot \text{toad}}$
8) $\sqrt{\text{rain} \cdot \text{cloud}}$
9) $\sqrt{\text{☆} \cdot \square}$
10) $\sqrt{\triangle \cdot \text{☺}}$

1) 6
2) 4
3) 8
4) 12
5) 12
6) 14
7) a
8) m
9) 9x
10) 14y

11) 3x
12) 10c
13) 11e
14) 6k
15) 12p
16) 7w
17) 9z
18) 10u
19) 8n
20) 14r

1) $\sqrt{8} \cdot \sqrt{5}$
2) $\sqrt{11} \cdot \sqrt{7}$
3) $\sqrt{m} \cdot \sqrt{p}$
4) $\sqrt{x} \cdot \sqrt{y}$
5) $\sqrt{15} \cdot \sqrt{r}$
6) $\sqrt{c^2} \cdot \sqrt{16} = 4c$
7) $\sqrt{\text{red}} \cdot \sqrt{\text{blue}}$
8) $\sqrt{\text{foot}} \cdot \sqrt{\text{hand}}$
9) $\sqrt{\text{☆}} \cdot \sqrt{\odot}$
10) $\sqrt{\text{☹}} \cdot \sqrt{\triangle}$

page 32

1) $2\sqrt{2}$
2) $2\sqrt{3}$
3) $3\sqrt{2}$
4) $2\sqrt{5}$
5) $4\sqrt{2}$
6) $3\sqrt{5}$
7) $5\sqrt{2}$
8) $2\sqrt{13}$
9) $2\sqrt{15}$
10) $3\sqrt{7}$

11) $6\sqrt{2}$
12) $5\sqrt{3}$
13) $4\sqrt{5}$
14) $3\sqrt{10}$
15) $4\sqrt{6}$
16) $7\sqrt{2}$
17) $8\sqrt{2}$
18) $3\sqrt{15}$
19) $2\sqrt{34}$
20) $10\sqrt{2}$

21) 12b
22) 9ms
23) 8q
24) 11a
25) 6x
26) 3yk
27) 13w
28) 10ef
29) 14nt
30) 7r

31) $4w\sqrt{2}$
32) $2g\sqrt{3}$
33) $4v\sqrt{5}$
34) $3rp\sqrt{5}$
35) $5kg\sqrt{3}$
36) $3b\sqrt{7c}$
37) $3y\sqrt{2x}$
38) $4\sqrt{6u}$
39) $8\sqrt{r}$
40) 9s

41) $ab\sqrt{x}$
42) $p\sqrt{m}$
43) $6y\sqrt{x}$
44) $wd\sqrt{t}$
45) $9bc\sqrt{a}$
46) $2wz\sqrt{2}$
47) $2em\sqrt{5}$
48) $5pr\sqrt{3q}$
49) 8ta
50) $6ns\sqrt{6tv}$

1) True
2) False
3) False
4) True
5) False
6) False
7) True
8) True
9) False
10) True

1) 8
2) 15
3) b
4) w
5) 4m
6) 13a
7) hat
8) glove
9) □
10) ✧

1) $12\sqrt{6}$
2) $35\sqrt{15}$
3) $ab\sqrt{xy}$
4) $mu\sqrt{wv}$
5) $24\sqrt{ce}$
6) $kn\sqrt{40}$
7) $18\sqrt{tic \cdot tac}$
8) $56\sqrt{hot \cdot cold}$
9) $12\sqrt{\diamond \cdot \triangledown}$
10) $48\sqrt{\square \cdot \triangle}$

1) 32
2) 108
3) 245
4) 54
5) $y^9 a$
6) $b^9 x$
7) 25c
8) 36w
9) $5v^2$
10) $10p^2$

1) $\sqrt{\dfrac{18}{6}} = \sqrt{3}$
2) $\sqrt{\dfrac{a}{c}}$
3) $\sqrt{\dfrac{6m}{8n}}$
4) $\sqrt{\dfrac{arm}{leg}}$

1) 4
2) 3
3) 6
4) 2
5) x
6) m^2
7) 3a
8) $8w^2$

1) $\dfrac{\sqrt{8}}{\sqrt{15}}$
2) $\dfrac{\sqrt{m}}{\sqrt{n}}$
3) $\dfrac{\sqrt{mind}}{\sqrt{matter}}$
4) $\dfrac{\sqrt{\odot}}{\sqrt{\bigstar}}$

1) $\dfrac{3}{5}$
2) $\dfrac{5}{6}$
3) $\dfrac{9}{10}$
4) $\dfrac{11}{14}$

5) $\dfrac{m}{y}$
6) $\dfrac{\sqrt{x}}{4}$
7) $\dfrac{r}{\sqrt{15}}$
8) $\dfrac{c}{12}$

1) $\dfrac{3}{7}\sqrt{\dfrac{5}{9}}$
2) $\dfrac{2}{13}\sqrt{\dfrac{7}{10}}$
3) $\dfrac{a}{c}\sqrt{\dfrac{d}{q}}$
4) $\dfrac{m}{n}\sqrt{\dfrac{x}{y}}$
5) $\dfrac{1}{3}\sqrt{\dfrac{c}{r}}$

6) $\dfrac{z}{f}\sqrt{\dfrac{15}{7}}$
7) $\dfrac{3}{5}\sqrt{\dfrac{man}{board}}$
8) $\dfrac{sip}{cup}\sqrt{\dfrac{gulp}{glass}}$
9) $\dfrac{\triangle}{\square}\sqrt{\dfrac{\stackrel{\star}{}}{\odot}}$
10) $\dfrac{\triangledown}{\smiley}\sqrt{\dfrac{\diamond}{\blacklozenge}}$

1) $\dfrac{\sqrt{10}}{5}$
2) $\dfrac{\sqrt{30}}{6}$
3) $\dfrac{\sqrt{24}}{8} = \dfrac{\sqrt{6}}{4}$
4) $\dfrac{5\sqrt{2}}{2}$
5) $\dfrac{9\sqrt{5}}{5}$

6) $\dfrac{4\sqrt{7}}{7}$
7) $\dfrac{a\sqrt{12}}{12} = \dfrac{a\sqrt{3}}{6}$
8) $\dfrac{m\sqrt{8}}{8} = \dfrac{m\sqrt{2}}{4}$
9) $\dfrac{r\sqrt{15}}{15}$
10) $\dfrac{\sqrt{11c}}{11}$

11) $\dfrac{\sqrt{5e}}{5}$
12) $\dfrac{\sqrt{18x}}{18} = \dfrac{\sqrt{2x}}{6}$
13) $\dfrac{10\sqrt{5}}{5} = 2\sqrt{5}$
14) $\dfrac{y\sqrt{19}}{19}$
15) $\dfrac{\sqrt{16}}{8} = \dfrac{1}{2}$

16) $\dfrac{\sqrt{36}}{3} = 2$
17) $\dfrac{\sqrt{14n}}{14}$
18) $\dfrac{12\sqrt{5}}{5}$
19) $\dfrac{t\sqrt{22}}{22}$
20) $\dfrac{\sqrt{39}}{3}$

1) Original
2) Original
3) Factored
4) Factored
5) Original
6) Factored
7) Original
8) Factored

1) +3
2) +1
3) +2/7
4) −1
5) −4
6) +1
7) −1
8) +1.63

1) monomial
2) binomial
3) trinomial
4) binomial
5) binomial
6) monomial
7) trinomial
8) monomial
9) trinomial
10) binomial

1) 1, 2, 4
2) 1, 2, 3, 6
3) 1, 2, 5, 10
4) 1, 2, 3, 4, 6, 12
5) 1, 2, 4, 5, 10, 20
6) 1, 3, 7, 21
7) 1, 5, 25
8) 1, 2, 4, 7, 14, 28
9) 1, 2, 3, 4, 6, 9, 12, 18, 36

10) 1, 2, 4, 5, 8, 10, 20, 40
11) 1, 3, 5, 9, 15, 45
12) 1, 2, 3, 4, 5, 6, 10, 12, 15, 20, 30, 60
13) 1, 3, 5, 15, 25, 75
14) 1, 5, 17, 85
15) 1, 2, 3, 4, 6, 8, 12, 16, 24, 32, 48, 96

16) 1, 2, 4, 5, 10, 20, 25, 50, 100
17) 1, 11, 121
18) 1, 5, 25, 125
19) 1, 2, 3, 4, 6, 8, 9, 12, 16, 18, 24, 36, 48, 72, 144
20) 1, 2, 4, 5, 10, 20, 40, 50, 100, 200

1) 1, 2, 3, 4, 6, 12, p, p^2
2) 1, 2, 4, 8, x, y, z, xy, xz, yz, xyz
3) 1, 3, 5, 15, b, c, b^2, bc, b^2c
4) 1, 13, w, v, w^2, v^2, w^2v, wv^2, wv, w^2v^2
5) 1, 2, 4, 8, 16, p, q, q^2, pq, pq^2

1) 7
2) 3
3) 14
4) 12
5) 18
6) 8
7) 27
8) 10
9) 20
10) 23

1) 3m
2) 5
3) 4b
4) y
5) 14c
6) $6p^2$
7) ax
8) 6
9) 10xy
10) $8b^2c^2$

11) $7x^2yz$
12) $6ab^2$
13) 2
14) 1
15) $9k^2$

1) $4m(3m + 1)$
2) $5k^2(3k - 2)$
3) $7x(1 - 4x)$
4) $6(3 + w^3)$
5) $6x^2(4 + 3x)$
6) $8ac(2a - 3c)$
7) $6np(3m^2 + 5p)$
8) $2v^2(3ru - 2mp)$
9) $7wxy(2w - 3)$
10) $4abc(abc + 2)$

11) $4(3d^2 - 2d - 1)$
12) $5r(3r^2 + r - 2)$
13) $6x(y^2 - 3y - 2)$
14) $14ab(a + 2b + 3)$
15) $x^2(5 - 7x + 12x^2)$
16) $3mnp^2(2m - 5n + 3p)$
17) $9r^2t(9t^2 - 7t + 4)$
18) $27u^3(3v^4 + v^3 - 2)$
19) $2c^2e(3 - 4e - 6c)$
20) $4p^2q^2(9q + 11pq + 7)$

1) No
2) No
3) Yes
4) No
5) Yes
6) No
7) No
8) Yes
9) Yes
10) No

11) Yes
12) No
13) No
14) Yes
15) Yes
16) No
17) Yes
18) No
19) Yes
20) Yes

1) (+1, +4), (−1, −4), (+2, +2), (−2, −2)
2) (+1, −4), (−1, +4), (+2, −2)
3) (+1, +6), (−1, −6), (+2, +3), (−2, −3)
4) (+1, −6), (−1, +6), (+2, −3), (−2, +3)
5) (+1, +8), (−1, −8), (+2, +4), (−2, −4)
6) (+1, −8), (−1, +8), (+2, −4), (−2, +4)
7) (+1, +14), (−1, −14), (+2, +7), (−2, −7)
8) (+1, −14), (−1, +14), (+2, −7), (−2, +7)
9) (+1, +24), (−1, −24), (+2, +12), (−2, −12), (+3, +8), (−3, −8), (+4, +6), (−4, −6)
10) (+1, −24), (−1, +24), (+2, −12), (−2, +12), (+3, −8), (−3, +8), (+4, −6), (−4, +6)
11) (+1, +27), (−1, −27), (+3, +9), (−3, −9)
12) (+1, −27), (−1, +27), (+3, −9), (−3, +9)
13) (+1, +30), (−1, −30), (+2, +15), (−2, −15), (+3, +10), (−3, −10), (+5, +6), (−5, −6)
14) (+1, −30), (−1, +30), (+2, −15), (−2, +15), (+3, −10), (−3, +10), (+5, −6), (−5, +6)
15) (+1, +48), (−1, −48), (+2, +24), (−2, −24), (+3, +16), (−3, −16), (+4, +12), (−4, −12), (+6, +8), (−6, −8)

1) (+2, +2)
2) (−4, +1)
3) (−6, −1)
4) (+3, −2)
5) (−4, −2)
6) (−8, +1)
7) (+7, +2)
8) (−14, +1)
9) (+12, +2)
10) (+8, −3)
11) (+9, +3)
12) (−9, +3)
13) (−5, −6)
14) (+10, −3)
15) (+8, +6)

1) $(c + 1)(c + 3)$
2) $(m + 2)(m + 3)$
3) $(w + 2)(w + 4)$
4) $(x + 1)(x + 6)$
5) $(e + 2)(e + 5)$
6) $(m + 3)(m + 4)$
7) $(t + 1)(t + 7)$
8) $(u + 3)(u + 6)$
9) $(y + 4)(y + 5)$
10) $(x + 1)(x + 9)$
11) $(a + 3)(a + 7)$
12) $(b + 2)(b + 9)$
13) $(p + 3)(p + 8)$
14) $(m + 4)(m + 7)$
15) $(r + 5)(r + 6)$
16) $(p + 3)(p + 9)$
17) $(x + 4)(x + 8)$
18) $(m + 2)(m + 11)$
19) $(q + 3)(q + 10)$
20) $(c + 4)(c + 9)$
21) $(e + 5)(e + 8)$
22) $(r + 6)(r + 7)$
23) $(x + 5)(x + 9)$
24) $(b + 6)(b + 8)$
25) $(n + 7)(n + 8)$
26) $(p + 4)(p + 12)$
27) $(s + 6)(s + 10)$
28) $(x + 5)(x + 12)$
29) $(k + 6)(k + 12)$
30) $(c + 5)(c + 15)$

1) $(x - 1)(x - 3)$
2) $(b - 2)(b - 2)$
3) $(z - 1)(z - 4)$
4) $(u - 2)(u - 3)$
5) $(y - 1)(y - 5)$
6) $(w - 2)(w - 4)$
7) $(b - 1)(b - 6)$
8) $(k - 2)(k - 5)$
9) $(d - 3)(d - 4)$
10) $(w - 3)(w - 10)$
11) $(x - 4)(x - 9)$
12) $(m - 2)(m - 30)$
13) $(e - 3)(e - 20)$
14) $(g - 5)(g - 12)$
15) $(f - 6)(f - 10)$
16) $(k - 3)(k - 32)$
17) $(s - 4)(s - 24)$
18) $(n - 6)(n - 16)$
19) $(p - 8)(p - 12)$
20) $(x - 4)(x - 25)$
21) $(t - 3)(t - 9)$
22) $(u - 5)(u - 7)$
23) $(q - 3)(q - 12)$
24) $(v - 5)(v - 10)$
25) $(z - 7)(z - 8)$
26) $(r - 3)(r - 15)$
27) $(y - 6)(y - 12)$
28) $(a - 8)(a - 10)$
29) $(c - 6)(c - 15)$
30) $(d - 10)(d - 11)$

1) $(m + 9)(m - 3)$
2) $(b + 10)(b - 4)$
3) $(a + 11)(a - 5)$
4) $(z + 6)(z - 3)$
5) $(y + 7)(y - 4)$
6) $(c + 8)(c - 5)$
7) $(r + 9)(r - 6)$
8) $(f + 4)(f - 3)$
9) $(p + 5)(p - 4)$
10) $(x + 14)(x - 2)$
11) $(d + 7)(d - 4)$
12) $(w + 20)(w - 2)$
13) $(b + 40)(b - 1)$
14) $(e + 21)(e - 2)$
15) $(k + 15)(k - 3)$
16) $(v + 9)(v - 5)$
17) $(g + 48)(g - 3)$
18) $(f + 36)(f - 4)$
19) $(k + 24)(k - 6)$
20) $(u + 18)(u - 8)$
21) $(m + 13)(m - 3)$
22) $(t + 16)(t - 6)$
23) $(p + 20)(p - 10)$
24) $(m + 14)(m - 2)$
25) $(n + 16)(n - 4)$
26) $(d + 18)(d - 6)$
27) $(q + 20)(q - 8)$
28) $(c + 16)(c - 1)$
29) $(r + 22)(r - 7)$
30) $(s + 25)(s - 10)$

1) $(k + 2)(k - 7)$
2) $(h + 3)(h - 8)$
3) $(m + 5)(m - 10)$
4) $(x + 6)(x - 14)$
5) $(y + 8)(y - 16)$
6) $(z + 3)(z - 11)$
7) $(a + 2)(a - 13)$
8) $(n + 4)(n - 15)$
9) $(b + 3)(b - 15)$
10) $(z + 2)(z - 14)$
11) $(p + 3)(p - 12)$
12) $(m + 4)(m - 9)$
13) $(f + 2)(f - 18)$
14) $(q + 3)(q - 10)$
15) $(c + 2)(c - 15)$
16) $(e + 5)(e - 6)$
17) $(d + 1)(d - 21)$
18) $(r + 3)(r - 7)$
19) $(c + 5)(c - 17)$
20) $(d + 1)(d - 85)$
21) $(s + 1)(s - 15)$
22) $(b + 3)(b - 17)$
23) $(e + 6)(e - 20)$
24) $(t + 2)(t - 19)$
25) $(a + 5)(a - 22)$
26) $(f + 4)(f - 28)$
27) $(u + 8)(u - 14)$
28) $(g + 2)(g - 56)$
29) $(v + 1)(v - 125)$
30) $(w + 5)(w - 25)$

1) $+x$ and $+x$
2) $+x$ and -3
3) $+5$ and $+x$
4) $+5$ and -3
5) $+a$ and $+a$
6) $+a$ and $+6$
7) -2 and $+a$
8) -2 and $+6$

1) $k^2 + 5k + 6$
2) $m^2 + 6m + 5$
3) $v^2 + 10v + 24$
4) $d^2 + 5d - 24$
5) $u^2 + 12u + 27$
6) $t^2 - 4t - 45$
7) $e^2 - 8e - 20$
8) $w^2 + 7w + 6$
9) $f^2 - f - 72$
10) $x^2 - 14x + 33$
11) $g^2 - 21g + 90$
12) $c^2 + 16c - 57$
13) $s^2 - 24s + 140$
14) $b^2 + 7b - 78$
15) $n^2 - 26n + 144$
16) $x^2 - 10x - 75$
17) $c^2 + 4c - 117$
18) $t^2 + 19t + 48$
19) $r^2 - 24r + 143$
20) $d^2 - 14d - 95$
21) $h^2 + 7h - 98$
22) $k^2 + 30k + 216$
23) $v^2 - 23v + 42$
24) $u^2 - u - 182$
25) $z^2 + 3z - 88$
26) $p^2 - 25p + 144$
27) $a^2 + 7a - 120$
28) $q^2 + 6q - 187$
29) $r^2 - 25r + 156$
30) $y^2 - 37y + 340$

1) $(x + 5)(x - 5)$
2) $(m + 7)(m - 7)$
3) $(k + 10)(k - 10)$
4) $(w + 12)(w - 12)$
5) $(2c + 6)(2c - 6)$
6) $(3w + 8)(3w - 8)$
7) $(5y + 5)(5y - 5)$
8) $(4c + 2)(4c - 2)$
9) $(6n + 1)(6n - 1)$
10) $(2p + 3r)(2p - 3r)$
11) $(3xy + 4z)(3xy - 4z)$
12) $(a + b)(a - b)$
13) $(np + 2v)(np - 2v)$
14) $(5 + x)(5 - x)$
15) $(9 + 1)(9 - 1)$

1) m
2) 1/p
3) 1/xy
4) a
5) r
6) ce
7) 1/k
8) $1/p^2$

1) a
2) 3 and y
3) (m + n)
4) x
5) x and y
6) m
7) e
8) (s + t)
9) c
10) v and n

1) b
2) 5
3) 3
4) $\dfrac{p}{q} + 1$
5) 9 – d
6) y
7) $\dfrac{b + c}{3}$
8) $\dfrac{u}{v} + 1$
9) 7x – 1
10) rm

1) x + 2y
2) b + c
3) $\dfrac{3m + 5n}{2}$
4) $\dfrac{2}{u - 3v}$
5) 2s – 5t
6) $\dfrac{1}{e + v}$
7) $\dfrac{2w}{x + 3y}$
8) 3d – 2e + 5f
9) $\dfrac{p - 3q}{2}$
10) $\dfrac{5n + 2r - 6k}{3}$

1) $\dfrac{m + n}{2(b + c)}$
2) $\dfrac{1 - 2y}{2 - 3y}$
3) $\dfrac{d + 3f}{2d - 3f}$
4) $\dfrac{2(3n - r)}{3n + 2r}$
5) $\dfrac{4 + 5e}{3(2 + 3e)}$
6) $\dfrac{2 - 3m}{2(m + 4)}$
7) $\dfrac{2(a - 2c)}{2a - 3c}$
8) $\dfrac{rv - 2sq}{3xy + 4wz}$
9) $\dfrac{2(nr + 2st)}{3ns + 5rt}$
10) $\dfrac{2x + 3z}{3z - 4x}$

1) $\dfrac{3(g^2 - 2)}{g(g + 1)}$
2) $\dfrac{3y - 2}{y(2y + 5)}$
3) $\dfrac{2c(1 + 2c^2)}{4c^2 - 1}$
4) $\dfrac{2n + 3}{2n(n^2 + 1)}$
5) $\dfrac{2(3 - 4r)}{5(1 + 3r^2)}$
6) 2a + 6
7) $t^2 - 3t$
8) $3u - 4u^2$
9) 2z – 3
10) $2c^2 - 3d$

1) Yes
2) No
3) No
4) Yes
5) No
6) No
7) Yes
8) Yes
9) No
10) Yes

1) num.: 5, (d + g)
   denom.: 3, 5, 15, (d + g)
2) num.: n, (r + t)
   denom.: (r + t)
3) num.: 3, 9, (e + f)
   denom.: 2, 3, 4, 6, 12, e
4) num.: (n + p – r)
   denom.: r, (n + p)
5) num.: (s – t + v)
   denom.: (t + v)
6) num.: (x – y)
   denom.: w, (x – y)
7) num.: 2, 3, 6, m, m^2
   denom.: (u + m)
8) num.: 2, 4, (p – q)
   denom.: 2, 3, 6, (p + q)
9) num.: 3, (b + c)
   denom.: (b + c), $(b + c)^2$
10) num.: x, x^2, (y – z)
    denom.: (y – z), (y + z), $(y^2 - z^2)$

1) 1/2
2) 3/5
3) 1
4) 1/3
5) 3u/2w
6) 9
7) 1/6
8) x/y
9) 3/7u
10) $2c/d^2$

1) $\dfrac{x}{z} + \dfrac{y}{z}$
2) $\dfrac{a}{c} + \dfrac{b}{c} - \dfrac{3}{c}$
3) $\dfrac{n^2}{r} - \dfrac{r}{r}$
4) $\dfrac{ant}{spider} - \dfrac{mouse}{spider}$
5) $\dfrac{11}{21} - \dfrac{t}{21}$
6) $\dfrac{p}{z} + \dfrac{2}{z}$
7) $\dfrac{\bullet}{\star} + \dfrac{\odot}{\star}$
8) $\dfrac{c}{2} + \dfrac{d}{2}$
9) $\dfrac{3v}{2x} + \dfrac{2u}{2x} - \dfrac{4x}{2x}$
10) $\dfrac{k^2}{4} - \dfrac{4k}{4}$

1) $\dfrac{4}{d} + 1$
2) $1 + \dfrac{e}{c}$
3) $\dfrac{1}{x} - \dfrac{y}{x^2}$
4) $\dfrac{p^2}{q} - 1$
5) $\dfrac{a}{b^2} + 1$
6) $\dfrac{n}{r} - r$
7) $1 + \dfrac{k}{v} + \dfrac{w}{v}$
8) $\dfrac{u}{s} + \dfrac{t}{s} + 1$
9) $1 - \dfrac{y^2}{x^2}$
10) $1 + \dfrac{b}{a} - \dfrac{c}{a}$

1) Left side
2) Number term
3) Variable term
4) Right side
5) Variable
6) Number term
7) Left side
8) Variable term
9) Variable
10) Right side

1) $5a - 8 = 3a - 2$
2) $4k - 16 = 8k + 8$
3) $3p + 15 = 60 - 2p$
4) $7b + 17 = 4b + 32$
5) $28 - 5e = 40 - 6e$
6) $5m + 20 = 2m + 8$
7) $6q - 22 = 8q + 6$
8) $c + 15 = 6c - 20$
9) $3f = 6f + 15$
10) $7n - 26 = 3n + 6$

11) $9d - 11 = 6d - 5$
12) $5r + 11 = 2r - 19$
13) $12s + 14 = 6s + 20$
14) $30v - 100 = 26v$
15) $10y - 26 = 8y - 6$
16) $25 - t = 10$
17) $7w + 33 = 5w + 19$
18) $4z - 15 = -8z - 27$
19) $u + 21 = 4u + 60$
20) $-24x - 12 = 42 - 33x$

1) $x = 5$
2) $b = 8$
3) $r = -3$
4) $v = -7$
5) $n = 7$
6) $d = -5$
7) $k = 18$
8) $t = 15$
9) $e = 6$
10) $q = -4$
11) $m = -6$
12) $w = 7$
13) $y = 35$
14) $f = 12$
15) $c = -60$
16) $s = -48$
17) $a = +6$
18) $p = +11$
19) $u = +2$
20) $z = 3$

1) $2a = 6$
2) $3d = 6$
3) $4k = -24$
4) $5p = 45$
5) $3b = 15$
6) $e = 12$
7) $3m = -12$
8) $2q = -28$
9) $5c = 35$
10) $3f = -15$
11) $4n = 32$
12) $3r = -30$
13) $6s = 6$
14) $4v = 100$
15) $2y = 20$
16) $t = 15$
17) $2w = -14$
18) $12z = -12$
19) $3u = -39$
20) $9x = 54$

1) $a = 3$
2) $d = 2$
3) $k = -6$
4) $p = 9$
5) $b = 5$
6) $e = 12$
7) $m = -4$
8) $q = -14$
9) $c = 7$
10) $f = -5$

11) $n = 8$
12) $r = -10$
13) $s = 1$
14) $v = 25$
15) $y = 10$
16) $t = 15$
17) $w = -7$
18) $z = -1$
19) $u = -13$
20) $x = 6$

1) $a = 5$
2) $e = 12$
3) $r = -1$
4) $n = 13$
5) $b = -10$
6) $f = 4$
7) $k = 10$
8) $p = -5$
9) $c = 7$
10) $d = 8$

11) $m = -6$
12) $q = -5$
13) $v = -11$
14) $z = -12$
15) $u = 15$
16) $s = -9$
17) $w = 2$
18) $x = -20$
19) $y = 6$
20) $t = -17$

1) $q = 20$
2) $r = 8$
3) $v = 19$
4) $a = 6$
5) $p = -5$
6) $n = 15$
7) $b = -14$
8) $t = 9$
9) $u = 12$
10) $c = -4$
11) $e = 2$
12) $m = 7$
13) $x = -12$
14) $d = -8$
15) $y = 10$

1) $n = 3$
2) $a = 4$
3) $g = 10$
4) $p = 7$
5) $b = 5$
6) $r = 9$
7) $z = 15$
8) $x = 6$
9) $s = 12$
10) $c = 14$
11) $v = 8$
12) $d = 11$
13) $t = 7$
14) $e = 10$
15) $u = 15$

1) $m = +5$ or $m = -5$
2) $n = +8$ or $n = -8$
3) $3r - 4 = +13$ or $3r - 4 = -13$
4) $10 - y = +1$ or $10 - y = -1$

1) $a = +6$ or $a = -3$
2) $k = -3$ or $k = +11/3$
3) $n = -1$ or $n = -4$
4) $b = +2$ or $b = -4$
5) $r = +1$ or $r = -4$
6) $e = +2$ or $e = +6$
7) $c = +1$ or $c = -1/4$
8) $t = -1$ or $t = +5$
9) $d = +8$ or $d = -4$
10) $p = +5$ or $p = -3/5$

1) $v = -4$ or $v = -2$
2) $m = -2$ or $m = 6$
3) $u = 3$ or $u = 7$
4) $t = -8$ or $t = 4$
5) $s = -3$ or $s = -5$
6) $x = -5$ or $x = 9$
7) $k = 4$ or $k = 5$
8) $c = -12$ or $c = 7$
9) $r = -6$ or $r = -1$
10) $y = -2$ or $y = 11$

11) $w = 6$ or $w = 9$
12) $p = -7$ or $p = 1$
13) $z = -8$ or $z = -4$
14) $q = -10$ or $q = 2$
15) $n = -5$ or $n = 15$

1) $\sqrt{40} \approx 6.3$ cm.
2) $\sqrt{116} \approx 10.8$ inches
3) $\sqrt{169} = 13$ miles
4) $\sqrt{625} = 25$ feet
5) $\sqrt{306} \approx 17.5$ meters
6) $\sqrt{373} \approx 19.3$ inches
7) $\sqrt{466} \approx 21.6$ feet
8) $\sqrt{681} = 41$ yards
9) $\sqrt{3721} = 61$ lightyears
10) $\sqrt{629} \approx 25.1$ mm.

1) $\sqrt{5} \approx 2.2$ yards
2) $\sqrt{9} = 3$ meters
3) $\sqrt{144} = 12$ feet
4) $\sqrt{45} \approx 6.7$ cm.
5) $\sqrt{189} \approx 13.7$ mm.
6) $\sqrt{576} = 24$ inches
7) $\sqrt{64} = 8$ feet
8) $\sqrt{1600} = 40$ miles
9) $\sqrt{112} \approx 10.6$ yards
10) $\sqrt{32} \approx 5.7$ meters

A.

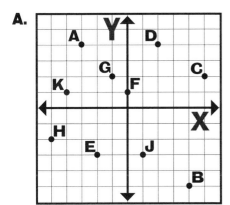

B.

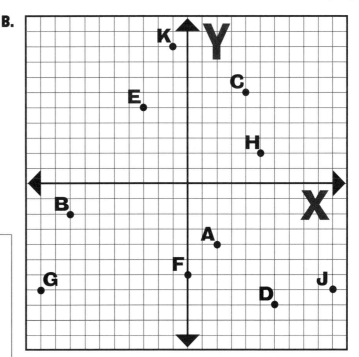

1) $x_1 = 6, y_1 = -8$
$x_2 = 7, y_2 = -4$

2) $x_1 = 1, y_1 = 4$
$x_2 = -5, y_2 = -6$

3) $x_1 = 3, y_1 = -7$
$x_2 = 3, y_2 = 11$

4) $x_1 = 5, y_1 = 2$
$x_2 = 9, y_2 = 2$

5) $x_1 = 6, y_1 = 9$
$x_2 = 12, y_2 = -4$

6) $x_1 = 7, y_1 = -1$
$x_2 = -6, y_2 = 14$

7) $x_1 = 4, y_1 = 6$
$x_2 = 1, y_2 = -3$

8) $x_1 = -2, y_1 = 1$
$x_2 = 2, y_2 = 6$

9) $x_1 = -3, y_1 = -8$
$x_2 = 4, y_2 = -9$

10) $x_1 = 0, y_1 = 4$
$x_2 = -6, y_2 = -10$

1) m = 1/2   3) m = 1/4   5) m = −1   7) m = 3   9) m = −10
2) m = −1   4) m = 2   6) m = 4   8) m = −2/5   10) m = 1

A.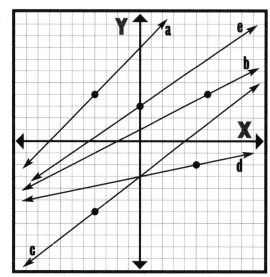

B.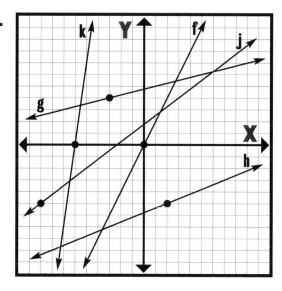

C.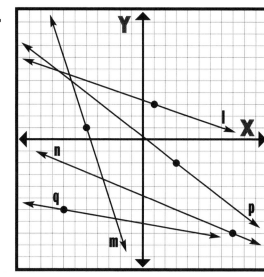

D.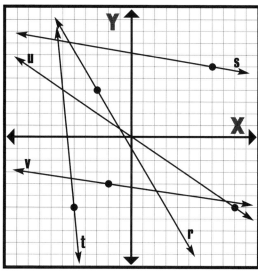

Coordinate Plane A:

a) x-intercept: x = −8
    y-intercept: y = 8

b) x-intercept: x = −2
    y-intercept: y = 1

c) x-intercept: x = 7
    y-intercept: y = 4

d) x-intercept: x = −5
    y-intercept: y = −7

e) x-intercept: x = 4
    y-intercept: y = −3

Coordinate Plane B:

f) x-intercept: x = 7
    y-intercept: y = 3

g) x-intercept: x = 1
    y-intercept: y = −1

h) x-intercept: x = −4
    y-intercept: y = −3

j) x-intercept: x = 3
    y-intercept: y = −6

k) x-intercept: x = −2
    y-intercept: y = 6

1) m = 3,   b = 8
2) m = −4,   b = 2
3) m = 1/2,   b = −4
4) m = 2,   b = 1/2
5) m = −3/5,   b = 3
6) m = 6,   b = 1
7) m = −8,   b = −4/5
8) m = 1,   b = −2
9) m = −9/10,   b = 3/2
10) m = 1/4,   b = 0

11) m = 7,   b = 2
12) m = −2,   b = −1/5
13) m = 1/8,   b = −6
14) m = −5/8,   b = 2/3
15) m = −1,   b = −3
16) m = 0,   b = 5
17) m = −2,   b = 1/2
18) m = 1/4,   b = 10
19) m = 1/6,   b = −4
20) m = −8,   b = −1

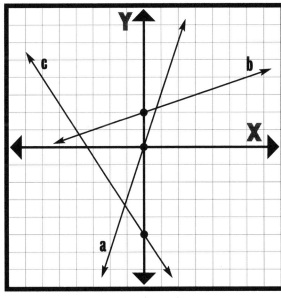

Lines a, b, and c

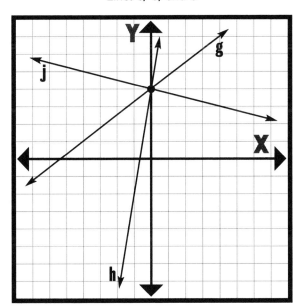

Lines g, h, and j

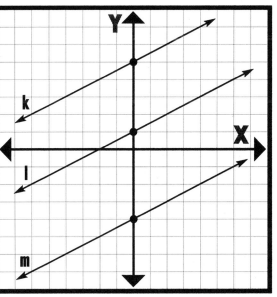

Lines d, e, and f

Lines k, l, and m

1) $y = 2x$

2) $y = \frac{3}{5}x - \frac{41}{5}$

3) $y = \frac{1}{2}x + \frac{11}{2}$

4) $y = -x + 5$

5) $y = \frac{1}{3}x + 9$

6) $y = 2x + 14$

7) $y = -3x - 6$

8) $y = \frac{2}{9}x + \frac{65}{9}$

9) $y = -2x$

10) $y = \frac{5}{8}x - 3$

1) $y = \frac{3}{2}x - 13$

2) $y = -2x + 9$

3) $y = -\frac{3}{2}x + 12$

4) $y = x - 7$

5) $y = \frac{2}{5}x - 3$

6) $y = -5x$

7) $y = 8x + 4$

8) $y = -\frac{3}{4}x + \frac{13}{4}$

9) $y = 3x - 2$

10) $y = \frac{5}{2}x + \frac{29}{2}$

1) $y = 2x + 6$
2) $y = 3x - 8$
3) $y = -3x + 2$
4) $y = x - 2$
5) $y = -2x + \frac{4}{3}$
6) $y = -\frac{1}{2}x + 2$
7) $y = -\frac{5}{7}x + \frac{5}{7}$
8) $y = 6x - 10$
9) $y = \frac{8}{3}x - 4$
10) $y = \frac{3}{2}x + 6$
11) $y = 3x - \frac{21}{5}$
12) $y = -x + 3$
13) $y = \frac{8}{5}x - 2$
14) $y = \frac{1}{3}x - \frac{1}{3}$
15) $y = -\frac{14}{3}x - 5$
16) $y = -\frac{1}{3}x + 3$
17) $y = 2x - 4$
18) $y = \frac{3}{5}x + 1$
19) $y = \frac{5}{6}x - \frac{8}{3}$
20) $y = -x - \frac{14}{3}$

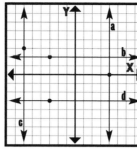

A.

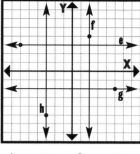

B.

a) $x = 4$ b) $y = 2$
c) $x = -6$ d) $y = -3$

e) $y = 3$ f) $x = 2$
g) $y = -2$ h) $x = -3$

1) $(-2, 5)$
2) $(9, 2)$
3) $(-1, -2)$
4) $(3, -5)$
5) $(1, -6)$
6) $(8, 22)$
7) $(3, 0)$
8) $(12, 1)$
9) $(-2, -10)$
10) $(0, 2)$
11) $(2, -2)$
12) $(2, 6)$
13) $(-3, 3)$
14) $(-10, 5)$
15) $(-3, -2)$
16) $(0, 8)$
17) $(-2, -9)$
18) $(5, -3)$
19) $(3, 10)$
20) $(2, 5)$

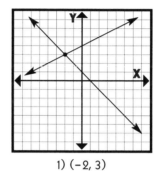

1) $(-2, 3)$

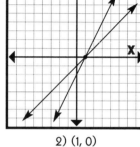

2) $(1, 0)$

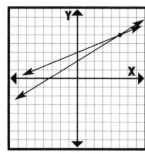

3) $(-1, 0)$

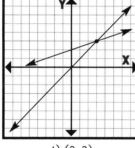

4) $(3, 3)$

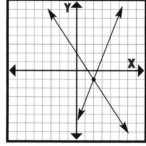

5) $(2, -1)$

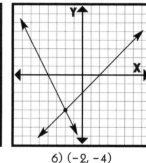

6) $(-2, -4)$

7) $(5, 5)$

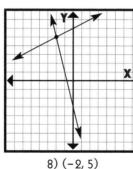

8) $(-2, 5)$

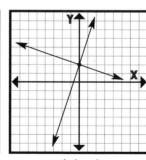

9) $(0, 2)$

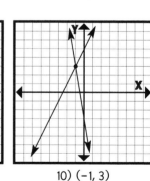

10) $(-1, 3)$

1) 5
2) 13
3) $\sqrt{113}$
4) $\sqrt{52} = 2\sqrt{13}$
5) $\sqrt{34}$
6) $\sqrt{40} = 2\sqrt{10}$
7) 10
8) $\sqrt{53}$
9) $\sqrt{185}$
10) 15

Answers

page 59

1) $n - 4$
2) $n + 8$
3) $n + 18$
4) $n - 18$
5) $n - 60$
6) $3n$
7) $-n - 7$
8) $-6n$
9) $3(3n - 5)$
10) $-4n + 10$
11) $-(2n - 3)$
12) $6n - 9$
13) $-6n - 9$
14) $6(n - 9)$
15) $9(3n - 6)$

1) $n + 8 = 3n$
2) $(n/100) \cdot 20 = 9$
3) $n + (n + 1) = 15$
4) $(n/100) \cdot 40 = 10$
5) $3(n + 2) = 21$
6) $2(n - 6) = -n$
7) $9 = (30/100) \cdot n$
8) $n = 3(2n - 5)$
9) $-(2n + 1) = 5$
10) $n + (n + 1) + (n + 2) = 33$
11) $6n/5 = n + 2$
12) $(n/100) \cdot 80 = 16$
13) $n + (n + 1) + (n + 2) + (n + 3) = 18$
14) $-4n = n + 10$
15) $30/n = n - 1$

page 60

1) $3n + 2 = 11$, so $n = 3$
2) $5(2n - 1) = 25$, so $n = 3$
3) $13n = 4(2n + 5)$, so $n = 4$
4) $4(2n + 6) = 2n$, so $n = -4$
5) $2n + 3 = -n + 6$, so $n = 1$
6) $4n + 6 = 3m - 8$, so $n = -14$
7) $4(-n - 8) = 3n + 3$, so $n = -5$
8) $7(4n - 20) = 8n$, so $n = 7$
9) $5(n - 6) = 2(n + 3)$, so $n = 12$
10) $10n - 4 = 14n$, so $n = -1$

1) 12 is 20% of 60.
2) 5 is 10% of 50.
3) 4 is 2% of 200.
4) 14 is 25% of 56.
5) 45 is 125% of 36.
6) 36 is 90% of 40.
7) 76 is 76% of 100.
8) 54 is 200% of 27.
9) 2 is 40% of 5.
10) 24 is 80% of 30.

1) 75 increased by 20% is 90.
2) 60 increased by 30% is 78.
3) 40 increased by 5% is 42.
4) 12 increased by 50% is 18.
5) 2 increased by 50% is 3.
6) 15 increased by 200% is 45.
7) 56 increased by 25% is 70.
8) 300 increased by 45% is 435.
9) 120 increased by 70% is 204.
10) 80 increased by 35% is 108.

page 61

1) 4, 5
2) 12, 14
3) 7, 8, 9
4) 8, 10, 12
5) 12, 13, 14, 15
6) 37, 39
7) 10, 12, 14, 16
8) 41, 43, 45
9) 15, 16, 17, 18, 19
10) 13, 15, 17, 19

1) Eli is 6 years old.
2) Zac is 10 years old.
3) Melanie is 13 years old.
4) Paul is 28 years old.
5) Asher is 21 years old.

1) $d = 45$ miles
2) $r = 9$ mph
3) $t = 2$ hours
4) $r = 12$ mph
5) $d = 300$ miles
6) $r = 20$ mph
7) $d = 24$ miles
8) $t = 5$ hours
9) $r = 13$ mph
10) $t = 2.5$ hours

page 62

1) Stacy's dad drives 24 mph.
2) The return trip takes 8 hours.
3) It takes Tony 3 hours.
4) The ski lift travels 600 feet per minute.
5) The boulder rolls down at 64 mph.

1) They will be 44 miles apart.
2) It will be 2 hours until they meet.
3) John's train is travelling at 65 mph.
4) They are 168 miles apart after 6 hours.
5) Jacob walks 6 mph.

1) Larger # − Smaller #
2) Smaller # − Larger #
3) Smaller # − Larger #
4) Larger # − Smaller #
5) Larger # − Smaller #
6) Smaller # − Larger #
7) Smaller # − Larger #
8) Larger # − Smaller #

1) Larger # = 12, Smaller # = 8.
2) Larger # = 13, Smaller # = 5.
3) Larger # = 12, Smaller # = 4.
4) Larger # = 14, Smaller # = 11.
5) Larger # = 16, Smaller # = 12.
6) Larger # = 23, Smaller # = 5.
7) Larger # = 16, Smaller # = 2.
8) Larger # = 15, Smaller # = 12.
9) Larger # = 14, Smaller # = 10.
10) Larger # = 25, Smaller # = 5.

1) Larger # = 20, Smaller # = 13.
2) Larger # = − 9, Smaller # = − 11.
3) Larger # = − 7, Smaller # = − 11.
4) Larger # = 13, Smaller # = − 13.
5) Larger # = 4, Smaller # = 1.
6) Larger # = 19, Smaller # = − 6.
7) Larger # = 15, Smaller # = − 13.
8) Larger # = 73, Smaller # = − 50.
9) Larger # = 200, Smaller # = − 100.
10) Larger # = 35, Smaller # = − 5.

1) Let s = Sam's # of apples;
   then 50s = Paul's # of apples.

2) Let z = Zane's distance covered;
   then (z + 30) = Kyle's distance covered.

3) Let e = Ethan's # of coins;
   then (e + 80) = Abigail's # of coins.

4) Let t = # of goals scored by Ted;
   then (t + 3) = # of goals scored by Ned.

5) Let j = Jacob's eating speed;
   then 3j = Daniel's eating speed.

6) Let m = Mason's # of points;
   then (m + 30) = Avril's # of points.

7) Let l = Liam's problem-solving speed;
   then 5l = Noah's problem-solving speed.

8) Let j = the # of calories Jack consumes;
   then (j + 1000) = # of calories that Shyan consumes.

9) Let a = Alexander's speed of energy gain;
   then 8a = Karyn's speed of energy gain.

10) Let s = Sophia's speaking speed;
    then 2s = Jayden's speaking speed.

1) Let b = Ben's height;
   then 5b = Ned's height.

2) Let p = balance in Paul's savings account;
   then 2p = balance in Ted's savings account.

3) Let s = Samuel's speed;
   then 3s = Jack's speed.

4) Let j = weight loss of Javier;
   then 3j = weight loss of Alexjander.

5) Let m = Madison's juice consumption;
   then 5m = William's juice consumption.

6) Let s = Sam's speed;
   then (s + 13) = Avril's speed.

7) Let z = # of "things" that Zombies eat;
   then 7z = # of "things" that Aliens eat.

8) Let s = Sophia's "Candy Crash" score;
   then (s + 5,000) = Isabella's "Candy Crash" score.

9) Let j = Juan's # of Facebook friends;
   then (j + 300) = Emily's # of Facebook friends.

10) Let a = Ava's daily average # of cups of coffee;
    then (a + 2) = Mia's daily average # of cups of coffee.

---

1) 5n
2) 10d + 5n
3) 25q + 5n
4) 50h − 10d
5) 25q − 10d
6) 5n + 50h
7) 5n − 50h
8) 10d − 25q
9) 5n − 10d
10) 10d − 5n

1) ME/E: value of dimes + value of nickels = $9.85
   ME/M: 10d +5n = 985

2) ME/E: value of dimes + value of half-dollars = $6.70
   ME/M: 10d + 50h = 670

3) ME/E: value of half-dollars + value of nickels = $96.65
   ME/M: 50h + 5n = 9665

4) ME/E: value of nickels + value of dimes = $8.80
   ME/M: 5n + 10d = 880

5) ME/E: value of quarters + value of dimes = $9.95
   ME/M: 25q + 10d = 995

6) ME/E: value of quarters + value of half-dollars = $2.75
   ME/M: 25q + 50h = 275

7) ME/E: value of dimes + value of quarters = $7.20
   ME/M: 10d + 25q = 720

8) ME/E: value of nickels + value of half-dollars = $93.35
   ME/M: 5n + 50h = 9335

9) ME/E: value of nickels + value of quarters = $32.95
   ME/M: 5n + 25q = 3295

10) ME/E: value of dimes + value of quarters = $102
    ME/M: 10d + 25q = 10200

---

1) 119 quarters, 129 nickels
2) 10 quarters, 19 dimes
3) 23 half-dollars, 30 dimes
4) 13 dimes, 20 nickels
5) 44 nickels, 53 dimes

1) 3 dimes, 21 nickels, 9 quarters
2) 7 nickels, 133 quarters
3) 5 half-dollars, 15 dimes, 30 nickels
4) 7 quarters, 14 dimes
5) 10 nickels, 80 dimes, 40 half-dollars

1) If n = # of nickels; (37 − n) = # of dimes.
   If d = # of dimes; (37 − d) = # of nickels.
2) If q = # of quarters; (89 − q) = # of dimes.
   If d = # of dimes; (89 − d) = # of quarters.
3) If q = # of quarters; (23 − q) = # of nickels.
   If n = # of nickels; (23 − n) = # of quarters.
4) If q = # of quarters; (71 − q) = # of half-dollars.
   If h = # of half dollars; (71 − h) = # of quarters.
5) If d = # of dimes; (10 − d) = # of pennies.
   If p = # of pennies; (10 − p) = # of dimes.

6) If p = # of pennies;
   (32 − p) = # of nickels.
   If n = # of nickels;
   (32 − n) = # of pennies.
7) If n = # of half-dollars;
   (98 − n) = # of pennies.
   If p = # of pennies;
   (98 − p) = # of half-dollars.
8) If h = # of half dollars;
   (13 − h) = # of dimes.
   If d = # of dimes;
   (13 − d) = # of half dollars.

---

1) 20 nickels and 55 quarters
2) 25 half-dollars and 28 dimes
3) 5 silver-dollars and 25 nickels
4) 25 nickels and 15 half-dollars
5) 35 nickels and 25 quarters

1) 5 questions, 4-point, long answer type;
   20 questions, 2-point, short answer type.
2) 15 bats; 5 packs of a dozen baseballs.
3) 5 bonus goals; 15 net goals.
4) 15 children's tickets; 25 adult tickets.
5) 5 sacks of rice; 7 sacks of flour.

1) MULTIPLICATION
2) TOTAL
3) ADDITION
4) TOTAL
5) ADDITION
6) MULTIPLICATION
7) TOTAL
8) ADDITION
9) TOTAL
10) MULTIPLICATION
11) ADDITION
12) TOTAL

1) MULTIPLICATION:
j = Jed's accuracy;
3j = Ned's accuracy.

2) ADDITION:
j = Jennifer's car's speed;
(j + 20) = Ken's car's speed.

3) TOTAL:
t = # trucks;
(13 − t) = # of cars.

4) MULTIPLICATION:
k = Karyn's throwing speed;
6k = Daryn's throwing speed.

5) ADDITION:
s = Sal's weight;
(s + 20) = Ben's weight.

6) ADDITION:
e = Evan's # of points;
(e + 25) = Todd's # of points.

7) MULTIPLICATION:
j = Joey's long jump distance;
2j = Arlen's long jump distance.

8) TOTAL:
s = Bo's # of science books;
(9 − s) = Bo's # of math books.

9) ADDITION:
m = # of goals Matt scores;
(m + 3) = # of goals Pat scores.

10) MULTIPLICATION:
m = Max's eating speed;
4m = Gwen's eating speed.

11) ADDITION:
h = Hal's score;
(h + 120,000) = Swen's score.

12) TOTAL:
w = # of windows;
(29 − w) = # of doors.

1) $d_1 + d_2 = d_T$

2) $d_1 = d_2$

3) $d_1 = d_2$

4) $d_1 = d_2$

5) $d_1 + d_2 = d_T$

6) $d_1 = d_2$

7) $d_1 + d_2 = d_T$

8) $d_1 + d_2 = d_T$

9) $d_1 = d_2$

10) $d_1 + d_2 = d_T$

1a) $d_1 = d_2$
1b) Let the variable stand for a time since the TIMES are unknown. Note, too, that the problem asks you to solve for a time.
1c) The unknown times are related by a TOTAL since the round-trip is given.

2a) $d_1 + d_2 = d_T$
2b) Let the variable stand for a rate since the RATES are unknown. Note, too, that the problem asks you to solve for the rates.
2c) The unknown rates are related by ADDITION.

3a) $d_1 + d_2 = d_T$
3b) Let the variable stand for a rate since the RATES are unknown. Note, too, that the problem asks you to solve for the rates.
3c) The unknown rates are related by MULTIPLICATION.

4a) $d_1 = d_2$
4b) Let the variable stand for a time since the TIMES are unknown.
4c) The unknown times are related by ADDITION.

5a) $d_1 = d_2$
5b) Let the variable stand for a time since the TIMES are unknown.
5c) The unknown times are related by a TOTAL since the time of the round trip is given.

1) Speed, home to bank = 5 hpm;
Speed, bank to home = 10 hpm.

2) Jed's rate = 8 kph; Ned's rate = 6 kph.

3) Ivan's speed = 18 kph;
Luke's speed is = 12 kph.

4) Rayna speed = 60 kph;
Leah's speed = 90 kph.

1) First friend runs for 5 seconds; second friend runs for 3 seconds.

2) Ken's speed is 2 yps; Ben's speed is 4 yps.

3) Graham drives for 5 hours; Janet drives for 3 hours.

4) Sandy drives 20 mph; her mom drives 80 mph.

1) Train 'A' travels 50 mph; Train 'B' travels 70 mph.

2) Sara's speed is 80 mph; Emma's speed is 65 mph.

3) The Yellow Lambo travels 3 fps; the Purple Ferrari travels 5 fps.

4) Ned's speed is 6 fps; Ted's speed is 10 fps.

1) Speed w/ tailwind = 776 mph; speed vs. headwind = 704 mph.

2) Speed w/ tailwind = 932 kph; speed vs. headwind = 838 kph.

3) Speed w/ tailwind = 637 mph; speed vs. headwind = 579 mph.

4) Speed w/ tailwind = 843 kph; speed vs. headwind = 735 kph.

1) $(-2, -1)$

2) $(-3, -6)$

3) $(5, -2)$

4) $(-7, -3)$

1) $300 = 1 \times (b + c)$
   $300 = 1.5 \times (b - c)$

2) $1{,}700 = 3 \times (p + w)$
   $1{,}700 = 4 \times (p - w)$

1) Speed of the plane in still air = 495 mph; wind speed = 55 mph.

2) Speed of the boat in still water = 27.5 mph; current speed = 2.5 mph.

1) Amount of treehouse built = $(1/6) \times (2) = 1/3$

2) Amount of cartoon animated = $(1/2) \times (1) = 1/2$

3) Amount of dinner cooked = $(1/3) \times (2) = 2/3$

4) Amount of room cleaned = $(1/60) \times (15) = 15/60 = 1/4$

5) Amount of song written = $(1/5) \times (4) = 4/5$

1) ME/E: Ashlynn's Fractional Work + Nadia's Fractional Work = 1
   ME/M: $(r_a \times t_a) + (r_n \times t_n) = 1$

2) ME/E: Candace's Fractional Work + Sarah's Fractional Work = 1
   ME/M: $(r_c \times t_c) + (r_s \times t_s) = 1$

3) ME/E: First Bird's Fractional Work + Second Bird's Fractional Work = 1
   ME/M: $(r_1 \times t_1) + (r_2 \times t_2) = 1$

4) ME/E: Man's Fractional Work + Daughter's Fractional Work = 1
   ME/M: $(r_m \times t_m) + (r_d \times t_d) = 1$

5) ME/E: Noah's Fractional Work + Adam's Fractional Work = 1
   ME/M: $(r_n \times t_n) + (r_a \times t_a) = 1$

1) x = 24/23 = 1 1/23
2) x = 12/13
3) x = 10/9 = 1 1/9
4) x = 30/11 = 2 8/11
5) x = 10/17
6) x = 18/7 = 2 4/7

1) It will take them 9/8 hours = 1 1/8 hour to finish the piñata.
2) It will take them 16/5 minutes = 3 1/5 minutes finish their pizza.
3) It will take them 35/3 minutes = 11 2/3 minutes to finish peeling.

1) ME/E: AC's Work + Window's Work = 1
ME/M: (1/2)h + (− 1/5)h = 1
or: (1/2)h − (1/5)h = 1

2) ME/E: Deborah's Work + Wind's Work = 1
ME/M: (1/1)h + (− 1/6)h = 1
or: (1/1)h − (1/6)h = 1

3) ME/M: (1/15)m + (− 1/50)m = 1
or: (1/15)m − (1/50)m = 1

4) ME/E: Zack's Work + Dog's Work = 1
ME/M: (1/45)m + (− 1/180)m = 1
or: (1/45)m − (1/180)m = 1

page 74

1) It will take 45 minutes to cool down the stage.
2) It will take 8 3/4 minutes for the tub to fill up.
3) It will take Justin 42 minutes to warm up the house under the given conditions.

1) You have 60 ml pure acetic acid.
2) The bottle contains 14 ml pure benzoyl peroxide.
3) There are .96 quarts pure citric acid.
4) The beaker contains 49.5 ml pure hydrochloric acid.
5) You have .65 liters pure lactic acid.
6) The bottle contains 21.6 ml pure magnesium hydroxide.

1) ME/E: lactic acid in 65% solution + lactic acid in 20% solution = lactic acid in 38% solution.
ME/M: .65 (14) + .20 (x) = .38 (14 + x)

2) ME/E: sodium hydroxide in 10% solution + sodium hydroxide in 85% solution = sodium hydroxide in 52% solution.
ME/M: .10 (40) + .85 (x) = .52 (40 + x)

3) ME/E: acetone in 80% solution + acetone in 45% solution = acetone in 60% solution.
ME/M: .80 (300) + .45 (x) = .60 (300 + x)

4) ME/E: citric acid in 75% solution + citric acid in 5% solution = citric acid in 15% solution.
ME/M: .75 (4.1) + .05 (x) = .15 (4.1 + x)

5) ME/E: Rubbing alcohol in 66% solution + rubbing alcohol in 20% solution = rubbing alcohol in 43% solution
ME/M: .20 (84) + .66 (x) = .43 (84 + x)

page 75

1) Suzana should add 1.31 liters of the 12% solution.
2) Caleb should add 5.90 cups of the 5% iodine solution.
3) Iris should add 4.5 gallons of the 92-octane gasoline.

1) Camille needs to add exactly 8/9 tablespoons of pure sugar.
2) Raquel needs to add 1.30 cups of peas.
3) Aimee needs to add 6.13 oz of gold.

1) Carl should take out 1.83 ounces of the current trail mix and replace it with 1.83 ounces of pure M&M's.
2) Astrid needs to remove and replace 5.90 milliliters of her 22%-white paint with pure white paint.
3) Ian needs to remove 3.24 cups of his first batch and replace it with the pure Darjeeling tea.

Preview of Algebra Survival Guide, 2nd Edition

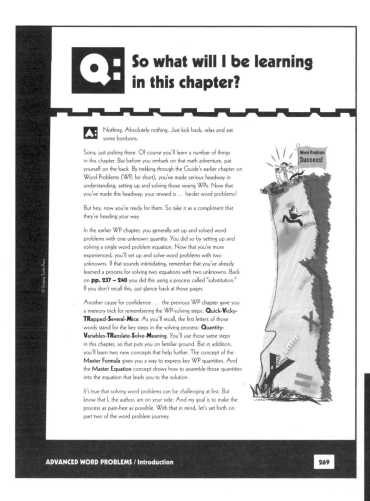

Q: So what will I be learning in this chapter?

A: Nothing. Absolutely nothing. Just kick back, relax and eat some bonbons.

Sorry, just joshing there. Of course you'll learn a number of things in this chapter. But before you embark on that math adventure, pat yourself on the back. By trekking through the Guide's earlier chapter on Word Problems (WP, for short), you've made serious headway in understanding, setting up and solving those vexing WPs. Now that you've made this headway, your reward is ... harder word problems!

But hey, now you're ready for them. So take it as a compliment that they're heading your way.

In the earlier WP chapter, you generally set up and solved word problems with one unknown quantity. You did so by setting up and solving a single word problem equation. Now that you're more experienced, you'll set up and solve word problems with two unknowns. If that sounds intimidating, remember that you've already learned a process for solving two equations with two unknowns. Back on **pp. 237 – 240** you did this using a process called "substitution." If you don't recall this, just glance back at those pages.

Another cause for confidence ... the previous WP chapter gave you a memory trick for remembering the WP-solving steps: **Quick-Vicky-TRapped-Several-Mice**. As you'll recall, the first letters of those words stand for the key steps in the solving process: **Quantity-Variables-TRanslate-Solve-Meaning**. You'll use those same steps in this chapter, so that puts you on familiar ground. But in addition, you'll learn two new concepts that help further. The concept of the **Master Formula** gives you a way to express key WP quantities. And the **Master Equation** concept shows how to assemble those quantities into the equation that leads you to the solution.

It's true that solving word problems can be challenging at first. But know that I, the author, am on your side. And my goal is to make the process as pain-free as possible. With that in mind, let's set forth on part two of the word problem journey.

ADVANCED WORD PROBLEMS / Introduction — 269

This being the 2nd Edition of the Algebra Survival Workbook, you'll also want to get the 2nd Edition of the Algebra Survival Guide to make your set complete. This and the next two pages offer a preview of selected pages from the new chapter in that book, the chapter on Advanced Word Problems.

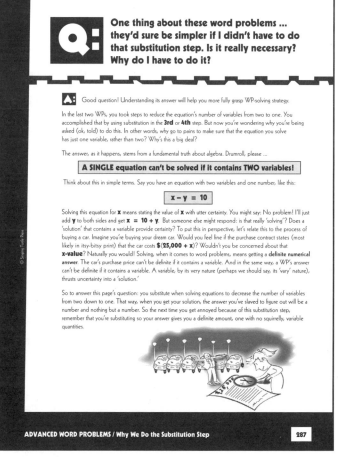

Q: One thing about these word problems ... they'd sure be simpler if I didn't have to do that substitution step. Is it really necessary? Why do I have to do it?

A: Good question! Understanding its answer will help you more fully grasp WP-solving strategy.

In the last two WPs, you took steps to reduce the equation's number of variables from two to one. You accomplished that by using substitution in the **3rd** or **4th** step. But now you're wondering why you're being asked (ok, told) to do this. In other words, why go to pains to make sure that the equation you solve has just one variable, rather than two? Why's this a big deal?

The answer, as it happens, stems from a fundamental truth about algebra. Drumroll, please ...

A SINGLE equation can't be solved if it contains TWO variables!

Think about this in simple terms. Say you have an equation with two variables and one number, like this:

$$x - y = 10$$

Solving this equation for **x** means stating the value of **x** with utter certainty. You might say: No problem! I'll just add **y** to both sides and get $x = 10 + y$. But someone else might respond: is that really 'solving'? Does a 'solution' that contains a variable provide certainty? To put this in perspective, let's relate this to the process of buying a car. Imagine you're buying your dream car. Would you feel fine if the purchase contract states (most likely in itsy-bitsy print) that the car costs **$(25,000 + x)**? Wouldn't you be concerned about that **x-value**? Naturally you would! Solving, when it comes to word problems, means getting a **definite numerical answer**. The car's purchase price can't be definite if it contains a variable. And in the same way, a WP's answer can't be definite if it contains a variable. A variable, by its very nature (perhaps we should say, its 'vary' nature), thrusts uncertainty into a 'solution.'

So to answer this page's question: you substitute when solving equations to decrease the number of variables from two down to one. That way, when you get your solution, the answer you've slaved to figure out will be a number and nothing but a number. So the next time you get annoyed because of this substitution step, remember that you're substituting so your answer gives you a definite amount, one with no squirrelly, variable quantities.

ADVANCED WORD PROBLEMS / Why We Do the Substitution Step — 287

Preview of Algebra Survival Guide, 2nd Edition

 OK, I get the Master Formula and Master Equation for mixture problems. But now I need to see all of the steps for a mixture problem put together. What exactly does that look like?

A: Here's a problem for which you can see all of the steps:

PROBLEM: Sid needs a solution that's 7% bleach to scour a dirty kitchen floor. He has 2.7 quarts of a 2% bleach solution, and he can add any volume of a 15% bleach solution to it. How many quarts of the 15% solution should Sid add to end up with a solution that's 7% bleach? Round answer to the hundredths place.

Steps	Example
1st) Name the **Q**uantity whose value you seek.	The volume (in quarts) of the 15% solution.
2nd) Set up a **V**ariable to stand for this quantity.	Let **q** stand for the number of quarts of the 15% solution that Sid will add.
3rd) Using the Master Formula, **TR**anslate the problem's three quantities from English to Mathlish.	2% solution: **.02 (2.7)** qts. of bleach 15% solution: **.15 (q)** qts. of bleach 7% solution: **.07 (2.7 + q)** qts. of bleach
4th) Write the ME/E in an abbreviated form.	Bleach in 2% solution + Bleach in 15% solution = Bleach in 7% solution.
5th) **TR**anslate the Master Equation from English to Mathlish by injecting the Master Formula quantities found in the **3rd** step.	⌐2%-Sol. Bleach⌐ + ⌐15%-Sol. Bleach⌐ = ⌐7%-Sol. Bleach⌐ ⌐.02 (2.7)⌐ + ⌐.15 (q)⌐ = ⌐.07 (2.7 + q)⌐

Steps	Example
6th) **S**olve the equation, following the steps in the Equations chapter.	.054 + .15 (q) = .189 + .07q .08 (q) = .135 q = 1.6875 q ≈ 1.69
7th) Say what the answer **M**eans.	This means that Sid needs to add approximately **1.69 quarts** of the **15%** solution to his **2%** solution to create the **7%** bleach solution.
8th) **CH**eck your answer by plugging the value you got for **q** back in, starting with the ME/E.	⌐2%-Sol. Bleach⌐ + ⌐15%-Sol. Bleach⌐ = ⌐7%-Sol. Bleach⌐ ⌐.02 (2.7)⌐ + ⌐.15 (q)⌐ = ⌐.07 (2.7 + q)⌐ .02 (2.7) + .15 (1.69) = .07 (2.7 + 1.69) (?) .054 + .2535 = .07(4.39) (?) .3075 = .3073 (??) But, rounding to the hundredths place, we get: .31 = .31 (!)

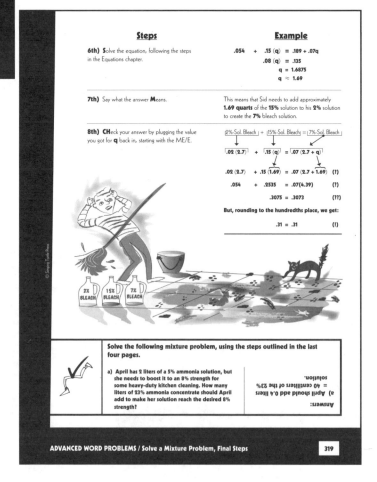

Solve the following mixture problem, using the steps outlined in the last four pages.

a) April has 2 liters of a 5% ammonia solution, but she needs to boost it to an 8% strength for some heavy-duty kitchen cleaning. How many liters of 23% ammonia concentrate should April add to make her solution reach the desired 8% strength?

Answers:

a) April should add 0.4 liters = 40 centiliters of the 23% solution.

CHAPTER TEST
Solve the word problems using the methods presented in this chapter.

PROBLEMS from FIRST HALF OF THE CHAPTER

1. The sum of two numbers is 97, and their difference is – 19. Find the two numbers.

2. Quianna has nickels, dimes, and quarters with a total value of $9.25. She has 8 more quarters than dimes, and she has 7 fewer nickels than dimes. Find out how many coins Quianna has of each kind.

3. Harry's Soup Kitchen needs to purchase tables, chairs and tablecloths for an outdoor addition that will be used in the summer months. Harry's needs to buy 8 times as many chairs as tables, and the number of tablecloths needed is four more than the number of tables. If the per-unit costs are $35 for tables, $18 for chairs, and $5 for tablecloths, and if Harry's spends $1,492 in all, how many of each item does Harry's purchase?

4. Dana and Raina are setting up their camp on a high desert plain. While they're setting up their tent, a curious skunk strolls through their campsite and startles the girls, who unfortunately, shriek. At that, the skunk sprays the campsite, and the girls dash off, Dana heading west and Raina heading east. If Raina runs 2 yards per second faster than Dana, and the girls are 84 yards apart after 6 seconds, how fast do Dana and Raina run?

PROBLEMS from SECOND HALF OF THE CHAPTER

5. College students are racing their rowboats along the Charles River in Massachusetts. Each team first rows upstream, against the current, and then turns around and races downstream, with the current. The course is 2 miles each way, for a total distance of 4 miles both ways. The Starched-Collar Team takes 1/2 hour to go upstream and 1/4 hour to go downstream. Given these times, what is the Starched-Collar Team's rowing speed in still water? And what is the speed of the current?

6. Solve each of the following problems:

    a) $1/8\, a + 1/6\, a = 1$

    b) $7/10\, v - 4/15\, v = 1$

7. Kelly can design an app in just 3 days, while her friend, Nelly, needs 4 days to design an app. If Nelly gets a two-day headstart on the process, and then she and Nelly finish the job working together, how long will it take the two young ladies to finish designing the app?

 Q: Now that I'm done, what are the main things I should be taking away from this chapter?

A: Hopefully there are two main things you should have learned: **1)** the overall process for solving word problems, and **2)** the steps for solving several specific algebraic word problems.

In terms of the overall process, you learned that in any WP you must carefully analyze the unknowns so you can set up variables and variable expressions to stand for the unknowns. You also learned that if you know both the Master Formula and the Master Equation for word problems, you'll be able to set up the quantities and the equation that you need to solve the word problem. In this respect, the Master Formulas and Master Equations are critical keys for WP success. To help you learn and memorize the Master Formulas and Master Equations for the WPs in this section, here's a table summarizing the key info.

Mathematical Expression or Equation

		MASTER FORMULA	**MASTER EQUATION**	**MASTER EQUATION ABBREVIATED**
T y p e	**COIN PROBLEM**	Value of Several Coins of the Same Kind = (Value per Coin) x (# of Coins)	(Value of Coin 1) + (Value of Coin 2) = Value Total	$V_1 + V_2 = V_T$
o f	**VALUE PROBLEM**	Value of Each Kind of Item = (Value per Item) x (Number of Items)	(Value of Item 1) + (Value of Item 2) = Value Total	$V_1 + V_2 = V_T$
W o r d	**RTD PROBLEM**	Distance = (Rate) x (Time)	Distance 1 = Distance 2 or Dist. 1 + Dist. 2 = Dist. Total	$D_1 = D_2$ or $D_1 + D_2 = D_T$
P r o b l e m	**RTD PROBLEM W/ WIND SPEED OR CURRENT SPEED**	Plane w/ wind: r = (p + w) Plane vs. wind: r = (p – w) Boat w/ current: r = (b + c) Boat vs. current: r = (b – c)	Plane w/ wind: D = (p + w)·t Plane vs. wind: D = (p – w)·t Boat w/ current: D = (b + c)·t Boat vs. current: D = (b – c)·t	D = (p + w)·t D = (p – w)·t D = (b + c)·t D = (b – c)·t
	WORK PROBLEM	Amount of Work Done = (Rate of Worker) x (Time Working)	(Fractional Work of Person 1) + (Fractional Work of Person 2) = 1 JOB	$FW_1 + FW_2 = 1$
	MIXTURE PROBLEM	Amount of Substance = (Percent Concentration) x (Volume of Substance)	Substance at Start + Substance Added = Substance at End	$S_{(Start)} + S_{(Added)} = S_{(Final)}$

Alignment of Algebra Survival Workbook to Common Core State Standards for Math

The tables on this and the next page show how the pages of the Algebra Survival Workbook (ASW) align with the **Common Core State Standards for Math**. The following abbreviations identify the sections of the ASW's pages:

P: ....Properties of Numbers
S: ....Sets of Numbers
P/N: .....Positive and Negative Numbers
O/LT: ...Order of Operations & Like Terms
AV: ......Absolute Value
EX: ......Exponents
R: ....Radicals

F: ....Factoring
C: ....Cancelling
EQ: ......Solving Equations
CP: ......Coordinate Plane
WP: .....Word Problems
AWP: ...Advanced Word Problems

Note: PASSIM means 'throughout'

Grade	CC Math Standard	ASW Section:	Pages of ASW
4	CONTENT.**4.OA.B.4**	F:	**39 (top set)**
5	CONTENT.**5.OA.A.1**	O/LT:	**13-17**
6	CONTENT.**6.NS.B.4**	F:	**37**
6	CONTENT.**6.NS.C.5**	P/N:	**7-12 (top set)**
6	CONTENT.**6.NS.C.6**	S:	**6 (bottom set)**
6	CONTENT.**6.NS.C.6.B**	CP:	**52**
6	CONTENT.**6.NS.C.6.C**	CP:	**52**
6	CONTENT.**6.NS.C.7.C**	AV:	**20 (top set)**
6	CONTENT.**6.NS.C.8**	CP:	**52**
6	CONTENT.**6.EE.A.1**	EX:	**22-29**
6	CONTENT.**6.EE.A.2**	WP: .... AWP:	**59-61** **64-75**
6	CONTENT.**6.EE.A.2.A**	WP: .... AWP:	**59-62** & **63-75**
6	CONTENT.**6.EE.A.2.B**	R: .... F: .... C: .... AWP:	**30** **36-38, 42** **43** **63-75**
6	CONTENT.**6.EE.A.2.C**	O/LT:	**15, 20, 21**
6	CONTENT.**6.EE.A.3**	P: .... CP: .... WP:	**5 (middle set)** **57** **61 (middle set)**
6	CONTENT.**6.EE.A.3**	AWP:	**66-75**

Grade	CC Math Standard	Section:	Pages of ASW
6	CONTENT.**6.EE.A.4**	P: .... **5** EX: .... **22-29** R: **30-35**	
6	CONTENT.**6.EE.B.5**	EQ: **47-51**	
6	CONTENT.**6.EE.B.6**	WP: .... **59-62** AWP: **63-75**	
6	CONTENT.**6.EE.B.7**	EQ: .... **48 (top set)**	
7	CONTENT.**7.NS.A.2.A**	PN: .... **12 (bottom set), 13 (top set)**	
7	CONTENT.**7.NS.A.2.D**	S: .... **6 (bottom set)**	
7	CONTENT.**7.NS.A.3**	PASSIM: P/N, EQ, WP, AWP	
7	CONTENT.**7.EE.A.1**	CP: **57**	
7	CONTENT.**7.EE.A.2**	WP: .... **60 (middle & bottom sets)** AWP: **63-75**	
7	CONTENT.**7.EE.B.3**	WP: .... **59-62** AWP: **63-75**	
7	CONTENT.**7.EE.B.4**	WP: .... **59-62** AWP: **63-75**	
8	CONTENT.**8.NS.A.1**	S:...................... **6 (bottom set)**	
8	CONTENT.**8.EE.C.7**	EQ: .... **47-50 (top set)**	
8	CONTENT.**8.EE.C.7.B**	EQ: .... **49 (bottom set)**	
8	CONTENT.**8.EE.C.8.A**	EQ: .... **57 (bottom set)**	
8	CONTENT.**8.EE.C.8.B**	EQ: .... **57 (bottom set)**	
HS	CONTENT.**HSA.SSE.A.1**	WP:.................. **59-62** AWP: **63-75**	
HS	CONTENT.**HSA.SSE.A.1.A**	R:........................ **30** F: .... **36** EQ: .... **47 (top set)**	
HS	CONTENT.**HSA.SSE.A.1.B**	F: .... **38-42** AWP: **63-75**	
HS	CONTENT.**HSA.SSE.A.2**	F: .... **38-42** C:....................... **43-46**	
HS	CONTENT.**HSA.SSE.B.3.A**	EQ: .... **51 (top set)**	
HS	CONTENT.**HSA.CED.A.1**	EQ: .... **47-51** WP: .... **59-62** AWP: **63-75**	
HS	CONTENT.**HSA.CED.A.2**	AWP: **63-75**	
HS	CONTENT.**HSA.REI.A.1**	EQ: **47-49**	
HS	CONTENT.**HSA.REI.B.4**	EQ: .... **51 (top set)**	

Also from Singing Turtle Press —

Check out Josh's blog @ **mathchat.wordpress.com**

Take a look at Josh's YouTube Channel at: **Josh Rappaport**

And here are some other titles by Singing Turtle Press

Now introducing ... Singing Turtle TUTORING

Singing Turtle Tutoring provides **ONLINE** tutoring services worldwide for all high school math subjects, and for the **ACT**, the newly revised **SAT** and the **SAT** Subject Tests.

To inquire about courses and services, visit SingingTurtle.com